Joint Ventures:
Stronger Together

By Ade Asefeso MCIPS MBA

Copyright 2015 by Ade Asefeso MCIPS MBA
All rights reserved.

First Edition

ISBN-13: 978-1508848110

ISBN-10: 1508848114

Publisher: AA Global Sourcing Ltd
Website: http://www.aaglobalsourcing.com

Table of Contents

Disclaimer 5
Dedication 6
Chapter 1: Introduction 7
Chapter 2: Understanding Joint Ventures 11
Chapter 3: Should I Start a Joint Venture? 15
Chapter 4: What Are My Chances of Success? 19
Chapter 5: What Are the Risks and Legal Implications? 23
Chapter 6: 10 Questions to Ask Before Committing to a joint Venture 27
Chapter 7: Joint Venture Negotiation 33
Chapter 8: The Secrets to Landing a Perfect Joint Venture 37
Chapter 9: Reasons Why Companies Go for a Joint Venture 41
Chapter 10: How to Convince Other Companies to Accept your Joint Venture Offer 45
Chapter 11: Five Things You Have to Consider When Opting for a Joint Venture 49
Chapter 12: Starting Up a Joint Venture 53
Chapter 13: Partial or Full Joint Venture 55
Chapter 14: Joint Venture Partner Search and Evaluation 61
Chapter 15: The Demands of Multiple Ownership 63
Chapter 16: Control of Joint Venture 67

Chapter 17: The Process of Securing Joint Venture Agreement 73
Chapter 18: Selection of Managers in a Joint Venture Alliance 77
Chapter 19: How Joint Ventures Can Work from a Marketing Perspective 83
Chapter 20: The 7 Deadly Sins of Joint Ventures. 87
Chapter 21: Avoid These 7 Joint Venture Killers. 93
Chapter 22: What to Do When Your Joint Venture Sours 97
Chapter 23: How to Create Win-Win Joint Venture 101
Chapter 24: Tips for Going Further, Faster with Joint Venture 107
Chapter 25: Advantages and Disadvantage of a Joint Venture 111
Chapter 26: Making the Most Out of a Joint Venture 115
Chapter 27: Examples of Joint Ventures 117
Chapter 28: Why Big Firms Form Joint Ventures 121
Chapter 29: Joint Venture Frequently Ask Questions 125
Chapter 30: Joint venture checklist 137
Chapter 31: Terminating a Joint Venture and the Consequences 141
Chapter 32: Conclusion 149

Disclaimer

This publication is designed to provide competent and reliable information regarding the subject matter covered. However, it is sold with the understanding that the author and publisher are not engaged in rendering professional advice. The authors and publishers specifically disclaim any liability that is incurred from the use or application of contents of this book.

If you purchased this book without a cover you should be aware that this book may have been stolen property and reported as "unsold and destroyed" to the publisher. In this case neither the author nor the publisher has received any payment for this "stripped book."

Dedication

To my family and friends who seems to have been sent here to teach me something about who I am supposed to be. They have nurtured me, challenged me, and even opposed me.... But at every juncture has taught me!

This book is dedicated to my lovely boys, Thomas, Michael and Karl. Teaching them to manage their finance will give them the lives they deserve. They have taught me more about life, presence, and energy management than anything I have done in my life.

Chapter 1: Introduction

A joint venture is when two or more businesses or people pool their resources and expertise to achieve a particular goal. The risks and rewards of the enterprise are also shared.

Reasons you might want to form a joint venture include business expansion, development of new products or moving into new markets, particularly overseas.

Your business may have strong potential for growth and you may have innovative ideas and products; however, a joint venture could give you.
1. More resources.
2. Greater capacity.
3. Increased technical expertise.
4. Access to established markets and distribution channels.

Entering into a joint venture is a major decision. This book gives an overview of the main ways you can set up a joint venture, the advantages and disadvantages of doing so, how to assess if you are ready to commit, what to look for in a joint venture partner and how to make it work.

A joint venture differs from a merger in the sense that there is no transfer of ownership in the deal.

This partnership can happen between goliaths in an industry. It can also occur between two small businesses that believe partnering will help them successfully fight their bigger competitors.

Companies with identical products and services can also join forces to penetrate markets they wouldn't or couldn't consider without investing tremendous resources. Furthermore, due to local regulations, some markets can only be penetrated via joint venturing with a local business.

In some cases, a large company can decide to form a joint venture with a smaller business in order to quickly acquire critical intellectual property, technology, or resources otherwise hard to obtain, even with plenty of cash at their disposal.

How does a joint venture work?

The process of partnering is a well-known, time-tested principle. The critical aspect of a joint venture does not lie in the process itself but in its execution. We all know what needs to be done specifically, it is necessary to join forces; however, it is easy to overlook the "hows" and "whats" in the excitement of the moment.

We will look at the "hows" in our review of the "Critical Factors of Success" later in this book. For the moment, let's keep in mind that all mergers, large or small, need to be planned in detail and executed following a strict plan in order to keep all the chances of success on your side.

The "whats" should be covered in a legal agreement that will carefully list which party brings which assets (tangible and intangible) to the joint venture, as well as the objective of this strategic alliance. Although joint venture legal agreement templates can readily be found on the Internet, we suggest you seek the appropriate legal advice when entering such a business relationship.

Chapter 2: Understanding Joint Ventures

As business generally becomes more globalised, the incidence of joint development is increasing. One factor influencing this trend is the changing nature of competition away from product and service towards the overall business model and supply chain structure. This is prompting companies increasingly to seek collaborative approaches to building a business, and it influences decisions and relationships in companies of all types and sizes.

There are five main mechanisms via which a business can be developed.
1. Go-it-alone.
2. Acquisition.
3. Merger.
4. Divestment and re-investment.
5. Alliance/joint venture

Let us look briefly at the rationale and requirements for each of the above mechanisms.

1. Go-It-Alone

The simplest mechanism for development of a company is via organic growth. This requires one or both of the following conditions.
    a) A growing level of demand, sustained over time.

b) Improvement of competitive position within a defined business, sustained over time.

An additional go-it-alone mechanism is via diversification. This requires some or all the following business conditions.
a) Unsatisfactory organic growth potential in core business(es).
b) Possible market diversification on the basis of product marketability.
c) Possible product diversification based on current or easily accessible technology.

2. Acquisition

The main reasons for undertaking an acquisition are as follows.
a) To improve competitive position by gaining market share and greater resources.
b) To reduce competition.
c) To diversify into new business areas if go-it-alone is not possible.

It involves persuading owners of a target business that their interests are better served by selling to an acquirer who is able to add more value than the current management team.

3. Merger

Merger is sometimes preferable to acquisition. It differs from acquisition in that one company does not buy the assets and goodwill of another but two or more companies form via agreement an integrated whole, such that the former individual companies combine and a new legal entity begins to operate. It is generally a lower-cost option than acquisition. It is particularly appropriate when products, markets and/or technologies are complementary thereby ensuring that synergies and economies of scale/scope can be achieved.

4. Divestment and Re-Investment

Divestment normally occurs when one or more of the following business conditions are encountered.
   a) Obsolescence of a product line.
   b) Demonstrable inability to manage part of a business portfolio effectively.
   c) Opportunity cost of remaining in a given business area when better alternatives exist.
   d) Unsolicited opportunity to sell part of the business portfolio at an attractive price.

5. Alliance or Joint Venture

These terms are often used somewhat imprecisely and misleadingly. Let us therefore start by distinguishing between types of alliance. I find it useful to start by thinking of two main types, and I term these 'partial' and 'full' alliances.

A partial alliance, of which there are a rapidly growing number in international business, does not in general affect the strategy of partner companies, but their operational performance. They are mostly relationships of convenience to take two types as examples.

a) Cost cutting or cost sharing by jointly using facilities.

b) Forming a consortium to undertake a specific contract or project or to share facilities/capabilities for a specific function, market or project. Often they are envisaged at the outset as being of fixed duration.

In contrast, a full alliance is concerned specifically with improving the competitive position of the partners in a way or to an extent or at a speed that is not possible by using other development mechanisms; because this type of arrangement is a central contributor to the future direction and competitive position, such an alliance is a key strategic option and is most often envisaged as a long-term undertaking. This is what can be termed a true joint venture.

Given, therefore, that there is no wholly satisfactory definition of the generalised term "joint venture", let us look for some characteristics.

A true joint venture is generally considered to be a full alliance in which an independent entity is created, involving two or more partners. The concept of an entity; an organisational form having separate structure and identity from the participating partners is central to the joint venture concept and differentiates it from other types of collaborative relationship.

Chapter 3: Should I Start a Joint Venture?

There is no straight answer to this question. The decision involves addressing various elements. Consider the following questions, so that you can constantly address and answer those important elements before and as you move forward.

1. What do I sell, and how do I reach my target market?

2. Who are my competitors? If they are better at generating revenues and reaching the marketplace than me, what do they have that I don't?

3. Are there geographical areas that will remain beyond reach without local partners, or acquisition costs that are simply too high?

4. Do I need to develop a know-how, which has already been developed by a company or by an individual?

5. Is there a logical business partner that could help me develop a vertical or horizontal market penetration?

6. Do I have all the human resources I need in marketing, R&D, production, or operations?

7. Is there a company I know which would have resources complementary to mine?

8. How do I feel about combining resources?

9. Do I like to lead by myself and act as a solitary business hero, or am I fine with sharing the pie?

10. Do I think it is better to own 20% of a $300 million company or 100% of a $2 million small business?

11. Do I have access to the right legal resources to structure the joint venture and insure all aspects are duly covered?

12. Are there local legal regulations I can bypass by partnering with a local business?

13. Do I have access to successful joint venturers who can share their experience with me?

14. Do I understand that going through the decision process entails sitting down and taking the time to write a full-fledged joint business plan?

15. Am I aware that in the vast majority of cases, merging activities, even when not necessarily identical, will result in an inevitable workforce reduction?

16. How do I feel about letting go of some of my most faithful employees?

17. Am I looking at partnering because I don't see another way out of my current business problems?

18. Do I already know of a person or a company that I see has a real interest in partnering?

19. Have I discussed this possibility with this person or with the person in charge of the targeted company?

20. If yes, what is the general feeling? If no, then it is time to start a high-level discussion to gauge the level of interest.

21. Is my company in need of more credibility?

22. Do I know of a potential joint venture target, which has the level of credibility I am seeking?

23. What are my strengths and weaknesses?

24. What are the threats and opportunities in my target market?

25. Do I have all the support I need to go through this major change in my business life?

26. If I am going through personal turbulences, does it make sense to start such a major project?

27. What are my chances of success?

Joint venturing should not be considered as a last resort action, but rather as one course of action among several others. This decision needs to be taken in a careful and methodical manner.

Chapter 4: What Are My Chances of Success?

Although there are no official statistics on the rate of success of specific strategic alliances, like joint ventures, per se, a few studies have, however, been conducted in this field. Their main findings were that most joint ventures fail about 60% of the time within five years. Why? Experts agree that the key to success is the human factor, such as human resources integration and knowledge sharing, rather than geographical or financial factors.

Keep in mind that joint venturing in third world countries entails a higher rate of failure. Lack of local legal knowledge, communication problems, divergence on agreed-upon objectives, differing deadline perceptions, etc., all contribute to this elevated rate.

How do we measure the performance of a joint venture?

There are several formulas that can be used. It depends on the strategic alliance in the first place. Do you wish to:
1. Increase profits?
2. Share R&D expenses?
3. Extend or maintain market position?
4. Improve distribution channels?
5. Reduce overall costs/economies of scale?
6. Develop new technology?

7. Diversify product offerings?
8. Reduce competition?
9. Spread risk (mainly on large investments)?

Some of those goals are easily translated into financial figures like "percentage of increased profits," "who incurs which expenses," and "increased product offerings." For example, if you were planning to increase your profits by 20%, you just need to compare your achievements with your previous situation, and you will know with certainty how well your joint venture performed.

Though some objectives are hard to quantify, like "reducing competition," for instance, methods are always available to analyze how well a joint venture's plan was executed. One could argue that if competition is cut down, then profits should increase.

If reducing competition has the sole objective of stabilizing or reversing a slowing revenue growth, it is easy to demonstrate the positive impact a strategic alliance could have on such a goal.

Remember, the key determining element responsible for joint venture failures is the human factor. Being able to make your employees feel comfortable about a potentially disturbing strategic alliance will be crucial to your success. This implies that not only must both sides understand how much they have to gain from this joint venture, but more importantly, how much they can lose by not partnering.

Information sharing will be vital, and it is essential that as early as possible, both teams talk and exchange their knowledge. This entails meetings, steering committees, joint company events, employee "swaps" and internal promotions.

Going back to our primary question; what are my chances for success? We know that on average, only about 40% of joint ventures are successful within five years. Since this figure includes partnerships with underdeveloped countries; which have a high rate of failure, we can reasonably state that if you join forces with a company located in a developed area and have done your homework, your probability of success should be closer to 80%.

Chapter 5: What Are the Risks and Legal Implications?

Because Joint Ventures are built on trust and convergent goals, one of the main risks you can face may occur if the partners are from different cultures. They may not trust operating a certain "way" or have divergent goals. Even with similar strategic goals, two partners who lack trust in each other may lack the willingness to reciprocate. When joint venturing, be prepared to give and take.

This sharing principle should govern the entire process. Many potential joint ventures, including large-scale projects, have died before the ink on the contract was dry, because of divergent goals and self-serving attitudes, which are not in synch with the essence of the joint venture. One example of this was the British Aerospace/Taiwan Aerospace alliance. After tough negotiations, the two parties signed an agreement during a celebrated ceremony in Taiwan. Soon after, Taiwan announced its wish to pull out of the deal. Why? Because their goals were divergent. Taiwan wanted to acquire new technology, which the British refused to give away, and the British wanted to capture new markets in Asia, which Taiwan refused to grant.

A joint venture concept is only effective when there is a true willingness to move forward together. Not even signed contracts have value if mutual trust and acceptance of the terms are not present. It is actually better not to consider a joint venture project if motives from either side are questioned by the other side. A graceful exit before any legal obligation takes effect will most likely prevent an inevitable failure. The risks involved are therefore simple to evaluate.

Even though these and other risks in joint ventures are present, the rewards can far outweigh pitfalls. It is important to completely evaluate your risks, and do your homework before and during the process.

The geographical locations of the partners and target markets involved will dictate the degree of legal complexity when joint venturing.

If you both operate in the United Kingdom, you will need to sign at least one document; a joint venture agreement; because of the rapid evolution of legislation, we strongly suggest that you seek proper legal advice, rather than using a pre-made template that is readily found on the Internet or in books.

If one of the partners is not located in the United Kingdom, or if both parties are foreign, additional documents will need to be signed; specifically, a New Legal Entity and a Joint Venture Agreement. Also, in some countries where local market access is restricted, you will have to go through a local "Validation" of your privileges and of the status of your joint venture.

Again, there are always legal variances depending on the goals and scope of your joint venture. I cannot stress strongly enough to go through the proper legal channels and seek comprehensive professional advice.

Owning a business can be one of the most exciting times in one's career. If done correctly, it can create the dream life you have always wanted. Depending on what you want from your business and how fast you want to get there, joining forces to create a more powerful presence in your market may be an attractive option.

Chapter 6: 10 Questions to Ask Before Committing to a joint Venture

Like a marriage, a joint venture often begins with enthusiasm and high expectations only to end in acrimony and legal proceedings. It is important to know as much as possible about a potential partner, including how his or her finances and family life may affect the business, before signing on the dotted line.

Here are some questions to ask before deciding if joint venture is a good idea.

1. What do I need from a business partner?

You should look for a business partner who brings something different to the table than you do. If you are creative, maybe you need a more detail-oriented partner. If you have money to invest in the business, you may want to look for a partner with access to a market, or with great connections. Or if you are shy, you might need a good "people person" to balance the equation. If they are similar to you, it might be more comfortable, but it may not be what you need. You need someone who complements your skills and personality.

2. What is your potential partner's financial situation?

It is important to have an understanding of someone's financial status and commitments before getting into a venture together. It is tough to ask what they are currently spending on a house or in payments to an ex-spouse, but someone's prior financial commitments shape the decisions they will make in the short term. If he has large outstanding obligations, but says he can get by on $28,000 salary, it is a red flag.

3. What are the potential partner's expectations on the time involved?

Partners don't have to spend the same amount of time, but it is important that they are on the same page as to each other's expected time commitments. How many hours a day does your partner expect to put into the venture, and do his expectations meet yours? It is equally important to level set your partner's expectations on your time commitments. The age old adage that it's better to under-promise and over-deliver applies here.

4. Is your potential partner's commitment to the business as strong as yours?

I don't care if it's a coffee house or a design firm, the business partner's commitment has to equal yours. A joint venture; especially one between friends can start off with fun and excitement, but within a short time, the slog of every day catches up with you. If they are not as committed to the business as you, they may lose their enthusiasm and may actually be damaging the brand every time you open your doors.

5. Is there something in your potential partner's family life that might make the business a secondary interest?

If your potential partner has a pregnant wife or is taking care of an elderly parent, he may be distracted from the business. That is why you have to be brutally honest when thinking of forming a joint venture. The partner can say, 'My wife is behind me 100 percent.' But I want to talk to the wife. "If they are too distracted by a family issue or their family isn't behind them, the business may be doomed from the start.

6. How would he or she handle a tough situation?

It's important to know what your potential business partner will do if he has his back up against the wall and it will happen. The best way to discover this is to look at what he's done in past business ventures. If he couldn't meet payroll, for example: Did he do the right thing and dip into savings or borrow from a credit card or a friend? Or did he pay employees late, or not at all? Or worse, did he skip paying payroll taxes? It all comes down to character issue. Payroll taxes are a Government obligation. If that is negotiable, you can bet your partnership is also negotiable.

7. What questions do they have for me?

If a potential employee doesn't ask any questions in a job interview, you might be less likely to hire him because of a perceived lack of interest. The same applies to a potential business partner, who should want to know about your character, reliability and expectations. I want them to ask me the same tough questions I ask them. If they say it doesn't really matter, it could mean two things: their expectations are too high or they might be kind of flighty. Things may be fine now, but in a month or two, they may want to change things or even get out of the deal.

8. What is the potential partner's standing in the community?

A lot of people seem good at first, but that may be their skill; seeming good at first. Once they get their foot in the door, it may be difficult to get them out. Talk to former employees to see what they were like to work with, or for. If you are looking for someone with money connections, verify that they have money. If they say they have great connections, see if those connections go beyond just being recognized and given a slap on the back. "A business partnership is not a marriage, but there should be some sort of courtship process that you can verify that they are who they say they are.

9. Are they willing to put everything in writing?

Many joint venture are cemented with a handshake, but this can be a recipe for disaster. It's crucial to put it on paper not only what is expected of each partner, but the consequences if expectations aren't met. There is something about actually putting it in writing that exposes the potential problem areas in the partnership. If someone has a family emergency and disappears the first six months of the business; even though it may not be through any fault of his own; are you still expected to give that person a certain percentage of the business? If someone simply isn't pulling his or her weight, you need to be able to get them out without destroying the business and if it's in writing, there is no arguing it.

10. Do I really need a partner?

If you can get someone to do something without giving them a stake in your business, it's always better. People get wrapped up in the idea of needing to work with someone, but it's not always a good idea. Sometimes you need somebody to show up from 9-5, work hard and go home. If you are cash poor, or it is a start-up and you don't expect to make money right away, taking on a partner might be the better option; but if you can just pay somebody to show up and work, it's generally a better option than giving them a stake in the company.

And now a bonus question....

What happens if we can't work it out?

Most people don't envision the rough times ahead for a new joint venture, so this question is probably the hardest to remember to ask at the beginning. Yet, the best time to address potential problems with your partner is at the beginning before emotions run high. You can't predict every potential problem, but a good start-up lawyer can help you work through some of the common problems and put a framework in place to help address unforeseen circumstances.

Chapter 7: Joint Venture Negotiation

How do you get what you want while leaving the other party feeling like a winner too?

Negotiating, when done correctly, creates strong win-win situations for both parties. Unfortunately, most ambitious professionals are stuck somewhere between emulating the stereotypical Hollywood idea of a hardball business tycoon and flashbacks to childhood memories of being told to be patient and wait for rewards. As a result, most professionals fear negotiating and treat it more as a guessing game or blackjack table.

You cannot advance your career or be a successful business owner if you avoid asking for precisely what you want or enter into negotiations without having a plan in place. With that in mind, here are five ways that you can quickly become a power negotiator.

1. Know exactly what you want

Identifying what you want before entering negotiations gives you the ability to both visualize the outcome and avoid leaving the table with the feeling of selling yourself short. Have an exact dollar amount, terms, etc. outlined on paper prior to meeting with the other party.

Once you identify your desired meeting goal, be prepared to ask for slightly more, allowing wiggle room for your boss or client to 'come down' to your desired price; however, don't be surprised if, using the next four tips, you actually walk away with more than your initial goal.

2. Understand the other party's position

What are their requirements and restrictions? Take the time to research the company and/or person you are meeting with and discover their surface needs, past negotiation outcomes, and what would make them look good. Remember that price is not always the most important factor, contrary to what the client or boss may say.

A close friend of mine was a hotel sales manager in his early twenties. One of the most valuable lessons his Director of Sales taught him was to offer what the competition cannot. As an example, his primary competition for large corporate conventions were two hotels nearby. His property had over fifty suites while each of the other hotels had less than fifteen. As a result, he would offer the meeting planners large quantities of complimentary upgrades for all of the company VIPs. Even offering a slightly higher room rate, he almost always got the business simply because the meeting planner jumped at the opportunity to look good by negotiating suites for company influencers. In the end, it wasn't about negotiating the lowest price, but the best deal for the company.

3. Know your value

What do you bring to the table? Are you offering a revenue-generating service to another business? If so, how much money will they make as a result of securing your services? If you are negotiating for a raise, understand if you have greatly outperformed past hires, making or saving the company a significant amount of money. How much would it cost the company to lose you?

4. Never accept less without gaining concessions

While you may not walk away with the exact dollar amount you envisioned, you can ensure that you leave with your desired 'value.' If you are seeking a 7% raise, but your boss informs you that the best the company can offer is 5%, consider requesting the ability to work from home one day a week or an additional five paid vacation days per year. Figure out an alternative option that is worth that 2% for you. Accepting less without gaining something in return is the equivalent of stating that you are worth less than your initial ask.

5. Be willing to walk away

Know your bottom-line and always be willing to walk away. While this can be difficult when dealing with large pieces of potential business or even a dream job, it is imperative that you never enter negotiations without the option to walk away. This lessens the likelihood of the other party being able to use hard-ball tactics to back you into a corner. Also, there will be times when you will need to state that their offer is not sufficient, and you don't think you will be able to do a deal. You may be surprised how often negotiations that seem to have broken down completely can be revived when the other party understands that you are not desperate, and that you have options.

Chapter 8: The Secrets to Landing a Perfect Joint Venture

Often joint venture can be inherent to a company's business model, for others they can play a role in customer acquisitions.

Yet, entrepreneurs, especially first-timers, are in a difficult spot when it comes to finding and negotiating potential joint venture. A young start-up or founder often lacks credibility or experience to negotiate a joint venture deal (or even score a meeting) with a Fortunate 500 company or other established businesses.

For those looking to secure a critical joint venture, here are five tips.

1. Show your product in action. A pitch or mock-up may be great ways to convey a concept, but start-ups can best overcome the credibility gap by demonstrating their idea in action.

Show your actual product, let people experiment with it or do a walk-through of your service. This requires more work, time and effort, but it ensures your vision is clear to potential partners and confirms you are fully committed.

2. Be strategic when targeting partners. Sometimes start-ups see the biggest potential partner as the only one worth pursuing.

This is a common misconception, as smaller or lesser-known companies can often be the best first partnerships. These "lower-hanging fruits" provide both credibility for future partnerships and help you work out product kinks in a lower-risk environment.

When identifying partners to target, be strategic in your thinking. Recognize who might be hungrier for a partnership or eager to innovate.

3. Realize the fear of missing out is real. The fear of missing out, is a real phenomenon that drives much social behaviour. Despite what some may claim, the fear of missing out is also prevalent in business.

Put yourself in the shoes of a business development person at a large company. Being the first mover in a partnership with a young start-up has many advantages if that start-up takes off. Often, these people want to be involved on the ground floor.

That said, big corporations are still taking a chance teaming up with young companies (brand risk and financial losses, to name a few). But if other partners are on board, the risk is shared, which may incentivize the corporation to join.

Take advantage of the fear of missing out phenomenon and shamelessly leverage your existing partnerships to build additional ones. Your first few partners may be extremely difficult to reach, but it gets easier.

4. Utilize your network for warm introductions. No matter what your start-up is or what partner you are looking to connect with, chances are that person receives hundreds of emails a day. While this doesn't mean cold emails don't work (they have many times for us), it does mean these emails can get lost in the fray.

So when possible, seek warm introductions from a friend or colleague. If you have a particular partner in mind, start scouring LinkedIn, alumni databases and other areas to find anyone who can make an introduction. If you find a mutual connection, send the person an explanatory email that can be forwarded on to the potential partner so your pitch is exactly what you want it to be.

5. Believe in yourself. Be confident in yourself and your product. When reaching out to partners you must be your biggest champion and your company's top evangelist. Keep in mind, if you don't appear to believe in your product, no one else will.

Chapter 9: Reasons Why Companies Go for a Joint Venture

Contrary to public perception, a joint venture does not only involve two people. It can actually involve more than two people. The meaning is the same as that of partnership in business except that "joint venture" is much more formal and official. It is actually a legal lingo that refers to the company or entity that is formed by the partnership of two or more people in order to start a business.

But joint ventures are very much popular to people as they are to established companies. This is because joint ventures provide benefits that can cut down costs and help make the job easier. For instance, market penetration.

With a joint venture, you will be sharing risk with each other as well as the profits of the business. All properties of the company or the entity created will be owned jointly and when the partnership ends or is dissolved, the properties will be divided equally unless otherwise stated of course in a legal agreement. A joint venture, however, can be long term or short term depending on the original agreement between the two parties. Often, there is no specified period of time, but rather a specified situation or goal.

Besides risk sharing, many people and even companies opt for a joint venture because of the benefits that they give to people. One of which is access and knowledge. One company for instance possesses a patent for a technology that another company needs to manufacture a product. Instead of paying for the patent, the two companies can agree to do a joint venture for a specific amount of time where they will manufacture the product and divide the profits equally while still keeping the idea and the patent to each company.

Another reason for companies to go into a joint venture is geographical limitations. For instance, if you have a company who wants to get into a country that has policies for foreigners owning their business, they can seek a partnership with a local company and provide that service. Some companies who have the language barrier to contend with for starting a business in a particular country can opt to partner with a local company instead to minimize the hardships of starting up a new company.

Market access is another reason why some people opt for joint ventures. Rather than spend millions introducing a product to the masses, a company can have a joint venture with a company who already has the market share and the access and just have that product or service bundled up with the local company's own product or service.

Joint ventures are also started when companies or people need the additional funding for the new business or for an expansion. Some lenders and banks also lend easier to companies that are in joint ventures because they feel that there is less risk involved with lending money to them.

Truly, joint ventures provide unending benefits to anyone but care must also be taking when choosing a partner. The success of a joint venture after all depends on how compatible the partners are.

Chapter 10: How to Convince Other Companies to Accept your Joint Venture Offer

Your company could be aiming to jumpstart or roll out an important project but you just could not easily do so because of the significant risks involved. Furthermore, your business may not have sufficient capital and technical expertise to carry on the endeavour. To be able to pursue your goals, you should form a joint venture with other companies, which should be willing to support and take part in your business initiative.

It may not be that easy to persuade other firms to get into an agreement to form a joint venture with your business. To be able to make the task less daunting and more successful, you have to follow the following tips and guidelines to make your joint offer to other businesses more interesting and more irresistible.

First, highlight the win-win situation your proposed project could bring about to partners. Make other companies understand about the practical and logical benefits that they could gain upon agreeing to get into the venture. You could also explain why you are determined to pursue it. Be honest to tell them that you aim to gain more revenues.

Do not produce very lengthy joint venture proposals. Remember the basic rule in business writing: Keep your message short, simple, and direct to the point.

Managers and owners of other companies could also be too busy to spend many minutes browsing through your formal joint venture offer.

Create an impression that you are a peer instead of a sales person. It helps to write a joint venture offer in a personal but detailed style. Making the proposal appear more personalized would do wonders. Do not shock the other companies or try to impress them through your showcase of technical knowledge and expertise. They may not fully understand some of the jargons and technical terms you use. As much as possible, make the copies more comprehensive but easily understandable.

Highlight your proposal to put more efforts into the joint venture. Prospective joint venture partners surely would appreciate it if you would assure them that they would be required to do less work. The less work the proposed project requires from them, the greater is the possibility that they would agree to become your joint venture partner.

Do not chase only the major players. You may be surprised at how capable less popular and smaller firms could be when it comes to managing and operating your proposed business project. It could be discriminating not to take seriously the minor and smaller businesses in the market. Smaller and minor players could provide you with more resources and expertise than the giants could do.

Tell them how your proposed joint venture could help their own customers and clients. All companies could not say no to projects that would make their loyal and important customers' lives easier and more enjoyable. This way, you could also actually help them provide much better services to their clients. Such a strategy is important in building trust in your joint venture.

Chapter 11: Five Things You Have to Consider When Opting for a Joint Venture

Joint ventures are great ideas for business but it is not without its disadvantages. Some fail while others crumble against the weight of the discord. So before you opt to go into a joint venture, here are some things that you have to consider in order to make sure that you will have a successful one.

1. Your partner

Your partner must be somebody or a company who you trust and believe in. If you are thinking of partnering with a company, research also on the owner as well as the person who is running the business. You will need to deal with these guys if you ever push through with the joint venture. The potential partner should also be able to go with the vision that you have for your company.

2. Their contribution

Another important aspect that you need to look into when starting a joint venture is the contribution that each partner will have for the project. The contributions should be made clear at the start of the project and should be written on paper if need be and signed by each of the partners. That way, everybody is made aware of their roles, thus minimizing the potential to slack off from their duties. It is also good to include in the document that if you ever slack off, any of the partners can be kicked out of the partnership or their shares can be reduced.

3. Exit strategy

There should also be something in writing until when the partnership will run. Remember that joint ventures are temporary but they can be in long term. It is good to have a specific date or period of run and then an option to extend for all parties. This will be a good way to ensure that everybody who is staying in the joint venture is still happy and is not just staying because the clause said so.

4. What the companies offer

Before you go around making an offer for a joint venture, make sure that you have thoroughly researched the company or the person that you want to be partners with. Check what they have to offer and make sure that they are the best in the field or that they can offer the product, technology or service that you need. Remember that you are only seeking the partnership because of that missing element and it is vital that you make sure that the missing element is really there.

5. Properties

When two companies go into a joint venture, they will be combining some of their assets. Make sure that the properties that each of you will be bringing to the table is equitable. It is not only in the number of properties but also the value attached to each one. If the contributions are not equal among the partners, make sure that you talk about it and put them in writing. Sharing of profits may depend on the contributions of properties. The bigger the contribution, the larger the percentage of your profits.

Chapter 12: Starting Up a Joint Venture

One of the problems with starting up a business or trying to enter a market is that sometimes you have the expertise but none of the money or you have all the capital but none of the manpower or the requisite knowledge. It's kind of risky when you are starting after all.

That is where starting a joint venture comes in. A joint venture is essentially a limited form of legal partnership that spreads the risk of a business between two or more partners. Joint ventures are usually dedicated to one purpose though there are several ventures that are continuing business relationships MSNBC, Microsoft and NBC Universal's cable news channel, being a prime example of an ongoing joint venture.

The lessening of potential loss for both partners is one of the more obvious perks of being in a joint venture, but the fact that you and your partner share resources and expertise is the main point. He may have information on the marketplace and already have a distribution channel set up, while you have a product that you think is appropriate for the target demographic and just needs to reach the customers. Combining your skills is a no-brainer.

So how does one go about going into a joint venture? Well, of course, the first step is getting a partner or partners. Write up a list of prospective partners and do a thorough screening; checking on the company's history and determining whether they are what you are looking for. After that, you should contact your potential partner so that you develop a business plan together; this includes both how your business relationship begins and ends, if your venture will be a limited one. Another part of the business plan will be how your companies will be structured to accommodate each other and how the income will apportioned.

When you have cleared up the nitty-gritty business details, it's time to go into the legal stuff. When you are dealing with the finer points of business law, it would be best to hire a lawyer – yes, it may be expensive, but it will be even more expensive in the long-run if you don't hire one to draw up your partnership agreement. An ironclad legal agreement is the best defence against any future litigation that can be sent in your direction. Here are the main points that should be highlighted in your joint venture agreement; how intellectual property rights are dealt with, how the venture is managed, what the partnership covers in terms of business and what each partner is supposed to contribute to the venture.

It should also be noted that the legal agreement must also cover how the venture may end; you may have achieved your goal, or you and your partners' interests have diverged or you have agreed to end the partnership at a particular time.

Chapter 13: Partial or Full Joint Venture

Is joint venture, partial or full, a last-choice option within business strategy?

No. In some circumstances it can be the only option. In others it can be the first choice. Joint Venture can become something of a "bandwagon", but there are circumstances in business development in which they produce better outcomes than those achievable by the partners separately. Let us consider the reasons for which joint venture is a strategically optimal mechanism for developing a business. The main ones are as follows
1. Minimising the risk of entry into a new market of developing an existing market further.
2. Achieving minimum size for operating in a market.
3. Overcoming legal constraints on operating in certain countries.
4. Pursuit of complementary interests and objectives.
5. Taking up a specific investment opportunity.

1. Minimising the Risk of Market Entry or Market Development.

In these circumstances the objective is to meet market entry costs on a shared basis, where solo entry would constitute an excessive cost to the business, thereby putting a significant part or even the whole of the business at risk.

This is a set of circumstances commonly encountered in:
    a) Entering a highly competitive, mature market.
    b) Entering a market in which the company has little or no experience.
    c) Developing a new product that is significantly different from the base-load business.

2. Achieving Minimum Size for Operating in a Market.

Linked to risk minimisation, there is a minimum operating size in certain product markets. Airbus Industry is an example of a joint venture set up to achieve minimum operating size in a world market with very few individual competitors. None of the partners in Airbus Industry could have contemplated entering the market for medium-sized airliners because of the minimum size required to take on the major competition - Boeing and McDonnell Douglas (whose civil aircraft interests were later acquired by Boeing).

The motor manufacturing industry is becoming characterised by joint venture. Examples of this are alliances between Mercedes Benz-Swatch in niche small cars and Ford-Fiat-Magirus Deutz in medium and large truck manufacturing.

3. Overcoming Constraints on Operating in Certain Countries.

In certain countries, especially socialist and developing countries, the full joint venture is often the sole means by which a non-native company may operate. These circumstances usually arise principally because of:
    a) Policy of a country to gain economic development leverage via technology transfer.
    b) Ideological/legal barriers to direct investment.

Both the above sets of circumstances have resulted in almost all the joint-venture activity that took place in China and the former Soviet Union plus its satellite countries until fairly recently. It remains the case in many developing countries that are concerned with promoting technology and know-how transfer to support economic and industrial development more generally.

4. Pursuit of Complementary Interests and Objectives.

Alliances between members of a supply chain (suppliers-manufacturers-customers) and also between direct competitors are used where there is a complementarities of interest to be pursued.

Compaq in its earlier stages is a particularly good illustration of this. Compaq Computers Inc was founded in 1982. Its rate of growth has been good. From the first day of its existence Compaq sought alliances with dealers, component manufacturers and software companies. By developing a complete package, Compaq was able to challenge IBM and others in personal computers and also gained a strong position in portable computers from an initial position of disadvantage. Compaq worked with Intel to design and incorporate a new type of microchip in a fast-developed new generation of portable computer.

5. Taking Up a Specific Investment Opportunity.

There is a form of joint venture that consists of one partner making a financial commitment simply as an investment opportunity and having little or no involvement in its management and development. The requirement of the investment partner is simply a financial one. Though this can be termed joint venture using our definition, it implies that one partner is taking the role of investment banker only. The managerial dimension of the relationship is absent. It is not a common form of joint venture, and is perhaps the least satisfactory from the strategic standpoint. It can give rise to problems if the investment partner subsequently attempts to get involved in the management of the alliance, particularly if the alliance is performing below target. The incidence of failure in this form of alliance is high.

Main risks and rewards of business development via the strategy discussed in this chapter.

Joint ventures are difficult to manage (this will be taken up in detail later in the book). Most people who have managed joint ventures consider the experience to be amongst the most testing of a career. Added to the normal challenges of managing a legal entity, there are specific problems arising from the fact of partnership between two or more differing organisations.

Main Risks

1. Culture clash between the participating organisations.

2. Lack of clarity about desired contribution of the alliance to the strategy of each partner.

3. Generation of unproductive cost, sometimes very rapidly if 2 above occurs.

4. A requirement for very talented management.

5. Divergence of strategy and objectives of partners during life of the joint venture.

6. Major shift in basic competitiveness of one partner during the lifetime of the joint venture.

Main Rewards

1. Rapid acceleration of development, especially in R&D activity.

2. Reduction of unproductive competition.

3. Tax benefits if structured carefully.

4. Entry into a market that would be too costly to enter solo.

5. Access to low-cost manufacture worldwide.

6. Risk reduction through spread in geographical coverage and financial commitment.

7. Further opportunities, especially in technology transfer.

Chapter 14: Joint Venture Partner Search and Evaluation

Stage One - Profiling the Required Partner

Time spent in preparation and analysis is time well spent when it comes to achieving success in setting up robust joint venture. The need to find and engage a committed capable partners or partners cannot be over-emphasised, but it is this aspect that in so many cases does not get sufficiently rigorous attention and the problems associated with this can lay hidden for a long time with potentially serious impact.

The first question is to define and quantify the potential contribution of the joint venture to one's organisations. What is the likely impact, financial and non-financial, on the organisation? What is the strategic rationale for the opportunity and how does it fit with the business strategy that one's organisation has been following and wishes to pursue in the future?

The next stage is to clarify the policy limits within which one's own organisation will agree to operate and the "hurdle rates" of performance that will be sought. This is needed in order to evaluate later the potential partners for compatibility in this area. At the same time the organisation needs to be clear as to the relevant resources that it brings to the opportunity and the additional resources that are needed. (Not least, part of this analysis should be undertaken subsequently by the possible partners to ensure compatibility.)

This analysis will give one's organisation a view as to the type of partner that will be needed to make the alliance work.

Stage Two - Evaluation and Selection

This leads directly from the final element of the "profiling" phase (partner definition).

Having established that joint venture is the best of the alternative mechanisms by which to develop the business idea and having set the basic characteristics sought in a partner or partners, screening criteria can be set up and prioritized, against which a long list of possible partners can be drawn up and refined into a short list. Naturally the more specific and differentiated is the opportunity, the briefer and more focused will be the long and short lists.

This part of the process is simple in structure and content but difficult in analysis and decision.

Chapter 15: The Demands of Multiple Ownership

As in the scoping/evaluation phase, achieving a balance between the needs of different partners is crucial to the ultimate success of joint venture once one moves into implementation and management.

The first set of questions relates to the expectations of the partners and in particular the capability of each partner to sustain costs over time before revenue stream turns the operation positive. Assuming that the collaborative option is the best of the alternative options for developing two or more companies, it is usually the case that the initial discussion of the deal focuses on how to share the proceeds. What is more important is to look at costs and timing and the impact of these two phenomena on the participating companies.

Put simply, the first part of the discussion should focus on the balanced contribution of each partner; the requirements in terms of return of/on capital and the time-scale for this; the minimum performance requirements in financial and non-financial terms. Each participant needs to view each venture as if it were an independent investor with hurdle rates that reflect not only its cost of capital but also the opportunity cost of pursuing the venture plus any risk premium that the venture should be required to accept.

These issues are frequently overlooked and a premature discussion takes place that results in a laborious route to agreement on profit share, with insufficient attention to the creation of profit in the first place.

Valuation of "sweat equity" or physical resource is a potential minefield, particularly when one partner is a fairly large company and the other(s) quite small or young. In these circumstances the smaller/younger partner(s) would often contribute in kind rather than in cash, particularly in units of human resource. This requires valuation and agreement early on.

Another area that is frequently neglected is the process for termination of the joint venture. It has been described as "planning for a possible divorce on the wedding day itself". Given the risks quantified in this book and in the event that the joint venture diverges from track to an extent that its continuation makes no business sense, a cost-effective wind-up process is needed so as to avoid further unnecessary expense.

The formal review process

Each venture will have an executive management structure at the operational level; however, a supervisory group rather along the lines of supervisory boards found in German industrial structures is useful in representing the interests of partners and to offer guidance, particularly in the early stages.

This is where the agreement of performance criteria and performance measures and the clarity of this agreement is paramount, since almost all collaborative ventures do not stick to the development path originally forecast. Review periodicity should be monthly in the initial phase, and then can gradually be reduced to a 6-monthly period. The focus should be on understanding and supporting the correction of variances rather than on directive management of the detail.

Quite simply, the role of the supervisory board is not to run the joint venture by "remote control" but to provide inputs and catalysis for the operating management team. Excessive parental involvement, though understandable, is a recipe for demoralizing the venture team.

Chapter 16: Control of Joint Venture

Collaborative operations require close but "light touch" approach to management on the part of the parent organizations. This framework can be summarized in six key points.

1. Parents should set only a few objectives that are clear and measurable.

What gets measured gets done. In the early stages the objectives and performance measures should be relatively few, unambiguous and easily measurable. Progress towards financial break-even with a time target should be a top objective. Revenue, cost reduction, time reduction, productivity, etc are examples of the type of simple, measurable objectives that necessarily should in the earlier stages take precedence over the "softer" measures such as customer satisfaction, product comparisons, customer mix. This is not to state that these issues are unimportant; it is to recognize priorities that are most likely to ensure success and stability of the venture.

2. A joint venture should set its own business strategy and operating plans.

Control freaks ought not to be involved in supervising a joint venture on behalf of a parent company. Successful ventures from projects up to full joint venture companies have in common a freedom to set their own plans and take full responsibility for their own destiny. Failed ventures share a characteristic; lack of "ownership" of business plans and repeated imposition of ever-changing directives from parent shareholders. Strategy and plans should always be subjected to presentation, discussion, modification and final approval by the supervisory team. This then constitutes commitment not only on the part of the venture team but also the parents.

3. Parents should review performance frequently in the early stages and then back off.

The best contribution that parents can make is to offer a "guiding hand" in the early stages and then to back off fairly quickly. Joint venture managers should be required to give early warning signals of variance or possible divergence from plan, but a parent company that acts like a gendarme guarantees a dead hand on initiative and potential success. Alliances and joint ventures are the ultimate form of delegation; the broad principles of delegation apply.

4. Parents should manage support not operational implementation.

The role of parents companies can be summarized as one of removing obstacles rather than getting involved in operational decisions.

Many collaborative ventures, particularly project-based ones, rely on inputs from one or more of the parent companies. Time is wasted if the management team of the collaborative venture is constantly arguing for inputs and transfers that ought to take place naturally. This and similar obstacles are the pressure points at which executives of the parent companies can make the most useful contribution to the venture.

5. Start-up usually takes longer than planned, but parents should set a maximum tolerable "sunk cost".

We see that even satisfactory joint ventures sometimes require financial re-structuring before ultimate success is achieved. The sunk cost dimension is one of the most difficult to deal with; a view that "we have put so much into this already and it will only take a little more......etc". At the outset there should be a clear view as to the maximum sunk cost that the venture can be allowed to incur before a decision to terminate is considered. Then the partners should move ahead unemotionally.

6. A joint venture should be allowed to operate as an independent entity.

This is just about the most difficult dimension in the management of a joint venture. Case experience points to excessively eager "parenting" as a frequent cause of disappointing joint venture performance and even outright failure. The first thing to accept is that parents should think of themselves as interested shareholders or venture capitalists not as venture managers; however, as risk takers, parents in this context have the right to influence the venture. The issue here is to identify the right type and quantity of influence that can best contribute to the venture. The answer is found in attitudes to operational management. The solution to this issue is to ensure that operational management in a collaborative venture has the confidence to seek guidance and input rather than end up needing it in a crisis. The best representatives of parents in working with a collaborative venture are executives who themselves have had prior experience in running a joint venture.

The issue of support not dirigisme.

Parent companies should see their role as supportive not interventionist, unless there is a divergence from plan that looks as if it could sink the venture. The least useful contribution that any parent can make to a collaborative enterprise, whether this is a simple agreement or a full joint venture company, is to try to micro-manage it. There are two main reasons for this.
- a) It would tend to demoralize the joint venture team
- b) It undermines the rationale for setting up a collaborative structure in the first place.

What experience and ideas do executives from parent companies have that they can share with management of a joint venture. Supporting management with ideas and shared experience rather than telling them what to do is a worthwhile contribution.

All the foregoing might give the impression that I am making out a case that management of joint ventures is different and more difficult than managing a single-owner operation. If so, good. That is what I hoped to do.

Divergence, positive or negative, is a different issue.

The only certainty about plans and forecasts is that they are most unlikely to turn out as originally expected, unless you are lucky. The big issue here is to recognize variance from the desired trend line and divergence from that line. Variance is to be expected in most instances; any joint venture will be above or below trend line but the question is whether it is actually on trend.

The performance of a venture may be underestimated or overestimated. The financial and operational implications are the same as for any commercial organization. Is it under-resourced in other words ought we to allocate more resources and revise upwards the assumptions and plans on which the venture was launched?

Alternatively is the joint venture heading for trouble in which case how do we get out with as little loss as possible? It is in both sets of circumstances that the position, resources, objectives and criteria of each parent company have to be considered carefully. It may be the point at which to alter the relativities in the ownership structure so as to take into account the different capacities and broader corporate objectives of the individual parents. Hard analysis and fluent decision-making are required in the above circumstances.

The management process for a collaborative venture should not differ radically from that of any single-owner operation.

Chapter 17: The Process of Securing Joint Venture Agreement

The process via which a deal can be reached in setting up a collaborative project (partial alliance) or joint venture company (full alliance) can be summarized as follows.

Objective conceptual and managerial robustness in the basic venture is insufficient to guarantee its ultimate success. The other element is to neutralize internal opposition to the venture in the first instance. It is very rare to undertake a collaborative relationship without encountering some measure of internal opposition in one or more of the partner organizations. Such opposition occurs mainly because the creation of the joint venture is almost always a response to an opportunity that partner companies cannot undertake alone and which therefore appears unusually risky. Moreover, collaborative ventures can be viewed as a threat to established structures and beliefs simply because often they are exactly that. In these circumstances it is not a good idea to pretend otherwise. Managing internal opposition is as difficult and necessary as managing the process of creating and running the venture itself. Dealing with this at an early stage is one of the most essential elements in securing later success.

It is, therefore, essential to ensure that a collaborative venture should have the overt support of senior executives in the participating organizations. Tacit top management "approval" with an inbuilt backsliding opportunity in reserve is a widespread feature of troubled collaborations. The processes relating to analytical and political considerations should be undertaken in parallel.

Other key issues centre on fluency in the process of gaining agreement. Successful collaborative ventures are not characterized by drawn-out discussion and protracted negotiation, with perhaps the only exception found in the case of major political involvement in very large-scale undertakings. If the idea is intrinsically robust then it ought to be obvious to the prospective partners. Lengthy wrangling over detailed minutiae of the basic agreement is almost always a predictor of trouble to come.

Types of collaborative relationships

It is useful to consider the different forms of collaborative initiative that are available. The requirement is to choose the optimal organizational form not the most obvious. The main ones can be broadly summarized as follows, with an example of each.
1. Informal or semi-formal agreement: "Ryanair recommends Hertz."

2. Project-focused alliance: Very large-scale civil engineering/construction projects.

3. Product-focused alliance Roche markets "Zantac" for GSK in USA.

4. Service-focused alliance: The three major global airline alliances.

5. Joint design-research-development: Philips/Sony in pre-competitive phase of DVDs.

Joint/parallel production: Fiat (I) and FSO (PL) "Cinquecento"

Cross-invested operations: KLM with NWA Joint marketing Airline/hotel/entertainment "packages".

Joint branding Credit Suisse First Boston (before CS purchase of FB).

Subcontracting Code share flying.

Licensing Anchor Malaysia brewing Guinness in Kuala Lumpur.

Franchising: Holiday Inn and several other hotel chains.

Supply chain linkages "Guest engineering" in many manufacturing sectors.

Joint venture company Airbus.

It will be seen from the above that it is not always necessary, or desirable, to form a joint venture company; there should be a clear strategic and operational rationale for so doing.

Choice - the correct option versus the obvious one

The choice of relationship can be critical. It depends on the depth of relationship that is required, and this ranges from a simple "gentlemen's agreement" to a fully incorporated entity.

Why incur the cost of setting up a joint venture company when a simple franchising operation could achieve better results quicker and cheaper? Several of the larger hotel chains operate very successfully using this mechanism, attracting owner-investors into the core business. In a different dimension, the growth of airline alliances is due as much to operational cost efficiencies than to marketing benefits, such as (a) the sharing of maintenance and terminal facilities with greater uptime and resource utilization and (b) economies of scale in purchasing components for increasingly homogeneous airplane fleets.

Chapter 18: Selection of Managers in a Joint Venture Alliance

There are four main points to bear in mind when selecting managers for this type of organizational structure. These are as follows.

1. Synergies do not occur automatically, even when the potential for synergies is obvious.

As with mergers and acquisitions, realizing the benefits of apparent synergies is a lot more difficult than is usually anticipated. Managers have to know how to make these happen clearly and quickly. Many things can get in the way of achieving synergies for which the collaborative venture was set up. Managers need to be aware of possible conflicts in marketing styles, extent of financial risk that can be borne, ethical standards in pursuing business objectives in alien cultures, and a host of other dimensions. It is dangerous to assume that synergies will be realized simply because it is clear that they ought to.

2. The human resource dimension is a critical success factor.

Whether the alliance involves a national or international operating structure, the question of human resources is often the most difficult, especially in the initial stages. The critical issue here is to ensure that whoever is leading the joint venture is aware of the cultural dissimilarities that characterize the members of the collaborative ownership. This can be as severe in a national as in an international partnership. We turn to this in the next two points.

3. Basic "technical" competencies are relatively straightforward.

The basic technical competences are no different in a joint venture than in a single-parent operation. Depending on the purpose and focus of the alliance, competencies such as marketing, finance, project management, production scheduling, etc are no different in an alliance from any other organizational structure.

4. Specific competencies relate to the "collaborative" and "joint" elements.

The specific challenges relate to the fact of multiple ownership, and these are manifest most strongly when there have been deficiencies in managing the process of creating the alliance. The main challenge is putting in place an effective system of communication and ensuring that it is implemented. It is clear that the communication channels must work for more than one parent, otherwise misunderstandings, errors and delays creep in with alarming speed and alliance managers are left spending too much time in picking up the pieces.

Specific competencies in the context of a collaborative venture

The specific competencies that relate to management of collaborative ventures are fourfold, as follows.

1. Dealing with more than one "boss".

As Director/General Manager of a collaborative venture the leader will have to work effectively with more than one "boss". No matter how effective is the process of delegation on the part of parents represented in the supervisory team, the fact remains that the nature of a collaborative venture is that its leader has to satisfy more than one boss. The skill required here is in ensuring that objectives, policies and performance measures are agreed on time lines that enable the venture to perform as if it were fully independent.

2. Balancing parental and local demands.

As with any business strategic and operational decisions are made under conditions of (often substantial) uncertainty. It is almost certain that in any collaborative venture the participating parent companies will have differing criteria in issues such as risk levels, investment 'hurdle rates' and internal transfer pricing, to identify just a few potential problem areas. All these issues should, as argued earlier, be part of the decision sphere of the collaborative venture itself; however this is a utopian wish. Effectiveness in gaining commitment of parents in a situation in which does not compromise business sense for the venture is crucial.

3. Creating effective communication systems.

Following naturally from the first two points above, the ability to create an effective communication system that keeps each parent 'in the loop' is something specific to collaborative ventures. Rather than providing every piece of minute operational data and decision to parents, the leader of a collaborative venture should communicate only (a) divergences from plan and decisions to bring the venture back on track and/or (b) advance warnings of events that could in the foreseeable future require input and guidance from parent companies.

4. Coping with two or more parent company cultures

Analysis of success and failure of collaborative ventures highlights the critical skill on the part of management in coping with differing cultures in stakeholder organizations. This issue is very often overlooked in the process of creating the collaborative venture and only surfaces at a later stage, often when difficult decisions have to be made on approaches to specific aspects of the business. Ideally the creation of a culture that is unique and appropriate to the collaborative venture itself is the proper solution to this issue; however, that is again utopian. To take an example, how, if at all, does a collaborative venture do business with unethical companies or repressive regimes when the position and policy of parent companies diverge on the issue? Assuming, as is too often the case, that this issue does not get addressed in advance, the leader of the joint venture has to be able to get parents with diverging views to reach a clear and quick decision.

Alliance management as part of a cohesive career path.

Avoid "sideways promotions".

Managing a collaborative relationship is not an activity in which a "sideways promotion" is an appropriate mechanism for appointing any level of management. It is an activity for top-class executives and should be a significant career development position. Top management in each of the parent companies should acknowledge that in addition to the skills required in business management there is another set of high-level skills that are particular to collaborative relationships, especially when one of more aspects of the relationship are international. This specific skill set is most significant when the organizational form has the characteristics of the more developed mechanisms; supply chain partnerships and joint venture companies.

Analysis of collaborative ventures that run into difficulties almost always points to management selection as a prime cause. Quite simply, a joint venture requires top performing managers. Even then success in a single company environment might not transfer if the additional competencies specific to joint ventures are not found.

Chapter 19: How Joint Ventures Can Work from a Marketing Perspective

Entrepreneurs have a variety of options when considering business strategies. I believe one of the most effective strategies to consider is a joint venture (JV). I think JVs are a natural fit for many entrepreneurs and they have certainly worked for me in the past and still working now.

As an entrepreneur, I think of my business as helping people (our customers) get what they want. In return, if my business does a fantastic job those customers will support my business and help it grow. When you think about it, a joint venture relies on the same concept. Help another organization get what it wants, while in turn you get what you want.

I have participated in a variety of JVs during my career and have found them to be good business strategies. I believe there are many benefits when creating a JV. You can take advantage of another company's existing infrastructure, intellectual capital, customer base, market reach, credibility and responsiveness. These are just a few examples of the tangible and intangible assets that can be gained by participating in a JV. There are certainly many more, but ultimately it's all about leveraging.

Let's say you create a breakthrough software program that helps retailers manage their sales but you don't have strong distribution channels. You can find reputable companies that supply products, equipment or consulting services to this industry and create JVs with them. This would open up your business to key target markets.

The possibilities that can be created with JVs are only limited by your imagination. Some common examples include joint ventures that focus on research and development, marketing, distribution, access to new markets, geographic reach, etc. The list can go on and on, although I wanted to show how JVs can work from a marketing perspective in this chapter.

Take the example of a friend of mine who developed and sells a high-end online training program to become a marketing consultant. He was looking to expand his business a few years ago and entered into a JV with a much larger company that sells training programs teaching people how to become a business finance consultant. The company generated thousands of leads a month and had a 7% sales success rate. My friend worked out a deal to have the larger company mail a letter he wrote to all the non-buyers (93% of the leads) at his cost and shared a percentage of the sales. These leads were all people interested in learning a skill; just not the exact one the company offered. He was able to gain access to the leads the other company generated at no cost. Both companies benefited because leads were not wasted and the larger company made additional profits with no additional expense while my friend made a killing with this JV. He always has many JVs in place at any given time.

I believe this example holds an important lesson for entrepreneurs. JVs can help you market your product and/or service to a larger audience by giving you access to another company's marketing resources and audience. In my experience, JVs that are structured properly also can help you reduce the time and cost of selling your product.

When considering a joint venture, I did recommend looking for established companies with a good reputation because partnering with that company will include a direct or indirect endorsement from them. That endorsement could carry a great deal of goodwill and break down sales barriers.

Even companies that may consider themselves competitors have created JVs because they understand that some aspects of their business could be stronger if they work together. A recent example is the video streaming site Hulu. A joint venture of News Corp NWSA -0.77% (which owns Fox), Disney (which owns ABC) and Comcast CMCSA -0.97% (which owns NBC) has been incredibly successful. The companies, which compete with one another on the TV airwaves, recognized that combining their programs for an online video service would be more powerful than if they each launched individual products. It's been a good bet and just this recently potential suitors to purchase Hulu have lined up with bids that approach $1 billion.

The examples discussed in this chapter emphasize the benefits of JVs and show success stories. Of course, some JVs don't work and it's not a strategy appropriate for every start-up. I advise entrepreneurs to seriously consider their need for a JV and the potential partner. As with everything, the devil is in the details. Before entering into a joint venture, entrepreneurs should ensure that they have consulted with their lawyer and that a JV agreement is in place.

Although it might not be the right fit for everyone, I have found participating in joint ventures to be a valuable business strategy and something I consider seriously in all of my business practises.. In-fact all of my businesses are joint venture.

Chapter 20: The 7 Deadly Sins of Joint Ventures

It's estimated at least 50 percent, and up to 70 percent, of joint ventures fail. Commit just one of the "seven deadly sins of joint ventures" and it's almost a guarantee that the project will become one of them.

The term "joint venture" covers a wide range of collaborative arrangements in which two or more businesses decide to share the costs, management and profits of a project that achieves a common goal. Successful joint ventures can offer tremendous rewards to entrepreneurs, but those that fail cost entrepreneurs a significant amount of time, money and frustration. Sometimes, even certain intellectual property rights are at risk.

Despite the many different types of joint ventures, the reasons they fail boil down to a common set of mistakes that partners make in the planning phases of a joint venture. Since these mistakes almost always doom the venture to fail, entrepreneurs should take great care to avoid the "Seven Deadly Sins of Joint Ventures."

1. Gluttony: Rapid consumption of capital. Many joint ventures use up their initial capital much faster than the partners expected. Partners who failed to plan for the possibility that resources may be consumed too quickly may then struggle to determine the best way to raise additional capital and rush into an unwise loan to raise funds. Prudent joint venturers will anticipate the need for additional capital and determine acceptable sources of funding in the initial joint venture agreement.

For example, the agreement may state that the venture may seek a third-party loan or a loan from one of the partners. The agreement may stipulate, however, that a loan from one of the partners must be on terms comparable to those from a third party.

2. Wrath: Arguments over control. Many joint ventures fail because the partners are accustomed to having control over their companies. Compromise about how to run the joint venture is a struggle.

As arguments erupt, the relationship may deteriorate until the partners can no longer work together. Joint venture partners should assume that there will be conflict. Appoint a board of directors with representatives from both companies to make decisions about how to run the venture. The board can then hire employees or contractors to manage the day-to-day operations.

The joint venture agreement should determine which decisions can be made by management and which decisions require approval from the board.

3. Lust: Desire for assets. In their lust for a partner's assets, entrepreneurs can make serious mistakes that may undermine the success of the venture. For example, an entrepreneur of a small technology company might agree to give a large corporation more control on the board of directors in exchange for a larger capital contribution. But in the long run, the entrepreneur may lose control over critical aspects of the venture, which could cause the venture to fail.

Partners in a joint venture should make sure that the assets each partner brings to the joint venture, such as intellectual property, capital or equipment, are appropriately valued and translated into reasonable shares of ownership and control.

4. Pride: Culture wars. Most entrepreneurs take great pride in the culture they have built in their company; but when two company cultures are combined into one venture, company pride can lead to unproductive arguments about using one company's methods over another.

For example, one partner may have a superior manufacturing process, but workers from the other company are reluctant to learn new methods, insisting that the old way is better. Joint venture partners should discuss in advance how they plan to handle cultural differences and, if necessary, train managers to help employees adapt to differences in company cultures.

5. Greed: Unrealistic profit expectations. Joint venture partners naturally want to see profits from the venture as quickly as possible, but distributing profits is rarely as simple as giving each party a share proportionate to their ownership. There will likely be a list of priorities to which distributions must be made, such as loan repayment or reinvesting a portion of the profits in the joint venture.

The joint venture agreement should lay out how and when profits will be distributed and the order of priority in which the profits will be distributed.

6. Envy: Competing partners. Many joint ventures are born from a partnership between two companies that operate in the same or similar industries to accomplish a specific project. As such, the competitive interests of the two companies can create a fundamental mistrust and envy between partners. That may ultimately cause the venture to fail.

The joint venture agreement should set specific boundaries regarding information that must be freely shared and information that may be reserved. If necessary, the agreement should also determine how one or both companies will restructure their operations to avoid any conflict of interest.

7. Sloth: Waiting to plan an exit strategy. During the busy planning phase of a joint venture, founding partners are often slow to plan their exit strategy, assuming that it can wait until the venture is up and running; but what happens if one party breaches the joint venture agreement? Or one partner is dissatisfied with the results of the joint venture and wants to leave?

Partners should, from the beginning of the joint venture, consider all possible scenarios in which the joint venture may end. The joint venture agreement should lay out the terms and conditions for a variety of end scenarios to avoid arguments down the road.

Joint ventures have the potential to be tremendously successful, but certain sins during the planning phases can have a deadly effect on the success of the venture. Entrepreneurs should take care with their partners to avoid these sins when creating their joint venture agreements. If a partner refuses to address any of these "deadly sins" in the initial joint venture agreement, consider finding another partner.

Chapter 21: Avoid These 7 Joint Venture Killers

Pitfalls abound when entrepreneurs decide to become partners. Know what they are ahead of time so you can set up guidelines that allow people to walk away if things go wrong.

From powerhouse financiers like Kohlberg Kravis Roberts to retailers like Baskin-Robbins to IT pioneers like Hewlett-Packard, business partnerships have been an important part of entrepreneurship and start-up success. The reasons are simple; complementary skill sets, shared equipment or expenses, and the idea that one person with "hard" money capital can create synergy with the intellectual capital of another person so both can profit from their venture.

In theory, joint venture is a great way to start in business. In my experience, however, it's not always the best way for the typical entrepreneur to organize a business.

The tough thing about most joint venture is that they are just like marriages, and if you know anything about those statistics, you know half of all marriages don't survive. Making a marriage work involves handling a volatile mix of partnership issues; ego, money, stress, monthly overhead and day-to-day expenses. Throw in some employees you must manage, and you have a good idea of the work required to make a business partnership successful.

If you are thinking about a joint venture, consider the following list and avoid the potential pitfalls:

1. Sharing capital instead of expenses: Whenever you share your own capital; be it money, resources, information or property; you automatically give away your enterprise ability. In a perfect world, the person you are partnering with is upright, full of integrity, and not at all tempted to take this gift and run with it as his own; however, the world is not perfect. So be careful. Instead, work out an arrangement where expenses are shared in an "associative" arrangement. It also makes it easier to walk away if things go wrong.

2. Partnering with someone because you can't afford to hire: This is a partnership killer right from the start. The scene is always the same; Bob has a business idea and Fred has the business skills, but Bob can't afford to hire Fred as an employee, so they decide to share duties, expenses and profits. What happens is both Bob and Fred end up working against each other, and Bob finds himself liable for Fred's obligations (financial and otherwise) under the partnership agreement. If you've got the idea and someone else has the skill, simply hire him or work out an independent contractor agreement. Don't give away what you don't have to.

3. Lacking a written and signed partnership agreement: Due to the nature of partnerships, every detail and obligation must be clearly defined and written out, and agreed upon by all parties. This is best done with a written legal agreement drafted by a well-qualified, mutually agreed-upon lawyer. Just make sure the lawyer is well-versed in business partnerships, and be sure to keep her card handy at all times. You may need that person again when things go wrong.

4. Overlooking a limited partnership: One of the main downfalls of a partnership agreement is the assumption of liability each partner makes for the other. A way around this is a limited partnership, where the limited partner is not liable for the actions or obligations of the general partner. Again, make sure an attorney well-versed in partnership agreements writes this arrangement.

5. Lacking an out or an exit strategy: Big-time marriages start with a pre-nuptial agreement. In business and contractual terms, a pre-nup is analogous to an exit agreement. In any joint venture agreement, define the terms of an exit strategy that allows you or your partner to walk away from the joint venture, or that provides options to buy out the other party. This can be done very clearly; simply and without imploding the operations of a successful business.

6. Expecting the friendship to outlast the breakup of the joint venture: Again, from the perspective of a marriage, how many ex-couples do you know who are truly friends? Not many, I suspect. So don't go into any joint venture with a friend expecting to remain friends after a joint venture breakup. It may sound great to do business with your friends, but remember, in the business world, it's always business first and friendships second. Also remember, most times when the business ends, so does the friendship.

7. Having a 50/50 joint venture: Every business, including joint venture, needs a boss. If you decide to go the joint venture route, make it a 60/40 or 70/30 split. Then you and the business have a point person for accountability and overall operational control. Also, keep your buyout or exit strategy clear and in your favour; benefitting you and saving problems down the road.

As a final note in this chapter, I leave you with an interesting solution to joint venture issue. Hopefully, it provides additional perspective.

When a company a friend of mine use to work for first considered partnering in the ice cream business, One of the companies was advised against it, thinking the compromises each company would make in getting the partnership to work would kill the product's potential. So the men each worked on their own businesses for two years before combining the two businesses under one name decided by the flip of a coin. Only after successfully launching and running their own separate businesses did the subsequent partnership actually work. That is one partnership formula I do know of that proved effective and if it worked for those two pioneers of retail success, it just may work for you.

Chapter 22: What to Do When Your Joint Venture Sours

When there is no more middle ground, a strong joint venture agreement can save you the hassles of an expensive legal battle.

Even in the best of circumstances, business partnerships can be fraught with conflict. To handle the twists and turns, smart co-owners put a well-drafted joint venture agreement in place to act as a road map. Without one, lack of guidance in the event of a dispute can result in a free-for-all for partners.

For partners who don't have an agreement, or even those who do, there are a few things they should consider in order to best protect themselves when conflict arises.

First, business partners need to evaluate whether they can mend fences and settle their differences. Difficult issues surface in all joint venture, and they can create stress in the business relationship, but if you work through these issues, you usually have a stronger joint venture.

It's important to figure out what is at the root of the friction. Ask, What is occurring within the joint venture that is causing you to make a decision to want to sell or liquidate? It can come down to rifts, family dynamics or other issues. How are those things affecting the business?

Business issues such as not making enough money, having too much debt or realizing your business model doesn't work; these are situations that may require you to adapt and change your business plan to make it work. Of course, fundamental issues that are hard to move past; lying, cheating, stealing or other illegal activity, for example; can be deal breakers and a legitimate basis to terminate the relationship.

Whether conflicts are resolved to make the partnership work is a business decision based in part on each partner's risk/reward tolerance level. Each partner should regularly assess the risks and rewards associated with their business to make sure they are in check.

To that end, ongoing communication and a periodic review of your partnership (especially the agreement, if you have one) is essential. Just as in any relationship, partnerships grow old and co-owners need to reassess how decisions are made, who makes what decisions, etc.

What do you do if you are unable to resolve your conflicts? At this point, business partners need to determine whether or not one partner buys out the other or both sell out to a third party. In the case of a partner buyout, the two important questions to ask are; who has the most passion for the business, and who has an immediate cash need that requires them to cash out of the business? As one would expect, both partners need to agree on the next course of action. In some cases, reaching an agreement may require a good business attorney to act as a sort of "corporate therapist."

Whatever the decision, make sure you hire a good business lawyer to help with the dissolution of the partnership. There is too much at stake to use your friend's uncle or some other attorney who is not an expert in business law. It is extremely critical that both parties either have their own independent valuations or that they agree on an independent business-valuation expert to determine the value of the business.

Most issues, serious or not, can be resolved at the onset through good communication and effective negotiation skills.

Chapter 23: How to Create Win-Win Joint Venture

I am often guiding my coaching clients how to have powerful conversations with potential partners so that they can be clear about what they want to gain and what they have to offer.

The ability for an entrepreneur to forge a strategic partnership (whether it is a business partnership, a joint venture or a short-term alliance) is critical for continued financial success in an ever-changing and highly competitive environment. Here are some tips.

1. See beyond what is on the table. Imagine there is one chocolate chip cookie on the table but everyone wants a piece. It's warm, chewy and calling you by name. OK, now imagine there is another whole sheet of cookies baking in the oven.

This is the best way I can describe the scarcity-abundance theory. The bottom line is that when we enter joint venture, the dynamic plays out best when we come from a place of abundance.

Sure, when we come together to create new joint venture, we can feel anxious and exposed. Take a deep breath and believe that all parties will eventually have their needs met to put you in the optimal position for achieving a better joint venture.

2. Be clear on your why. Often people enter into joint venture because they don't feel they have enough value on their own. Coming from this place almost never creates a mutually beneficial relationship. The chance of getting burned is almost guaranteed.

Be clear on the value you bring to the table. Be honest about why you are interested in creating a joint venture and what you bring to the table. Write down the answers to the following: "Why does this relationship benefit my professional and personal growth?" and "What do I expect to gain from this joint venture?"

This is not a time to hash out your business plan or a mission and vision statement. If you don't have clear answers to these questions, you are not in a position to create effective connections.

Do your homework. Do not pass "go" until you have these answers covered.

3. Understand the why of your potential partners. Do not hesitate to ask a potential partner why he or she is seeking to connect and what he or she is hoping to gain.

The answers are not always clear at the outset. Listen carefully to what the other party is saying. Do you have the right chemistry and a shared vision to make this relationship mutually beneficial?

If you sense resistance or a lack of clarity, postpone any decision making until your questions are answered completely and you are confident this relationship will be profitable and beneficial to you both.

4. Seek commonality and a shared vision. Do you see this partnership as boosting the vision of both sides? Do you share the same excitement and passion for what you do and how you want to grow?

Certainly everyone comes with different strengths and weaknesses, however, the best partnerships work because the vision and values are shared as well as passion and enthusiasm. These can carry the partnership through any sticking points in negotiations. Remember, the best partnerships work most smoothly when each party's strengths shore up the connection to create elevated and shared success.

5. Don't rush the process. There is no need to hurry into a deal. Sometimes enthusiasm and excitement can blind you to red flags and foibles. Set a follow-up meeting to address next steps so as to be sure that both parties are on board and equally committed. A lack of follow-through by one party could mean stress and strain in the future. Judicious and thorough planning are key.

6. Expect to be uncomfortable. When hashing out details about what each party brings to the table, expect some push and pull. A lot of people become uncomfortable with disagreement. Don't let that be you. By being prepared, you will be clear about where you stand firm and where you can give way. Negotiation is a dance and as the saying goes, it takes two to tango.

By holding on for a positive outcome, commit to moving through sticking points with grace and tact. Expect win-win relationships.

7. Write things down. Great partnerships require great protection. Seal all agreements in writing to avoid messy breakups in the future. This is one of the hardest conversations to have but by far the most important.

How many times have you heard about a partnership that started off rosy and blew apart with hard feelings and even costly results?

A great way to phrase this is to say, "I'm really excited about this partnership and I think we will achieve great success together; because I value our relationship so much, let's put our agreement in writing to protect our interests and ensure our growth as partners. How does that sound to you?"

Granting yourself some protection by signing on the dotted line is brilliance in action. Respect yourself enough to protect yourself and your ideas. Contracts preserve relationships not destroy them. If a possible partner bristles at signing anything in writing, thank your lucky stars and walk away. Integrity includes clarity of principle and an agreement in writing seals a relationship and provides a level of security and fairness that is priceless.

A written Joint Venture Agreement should cover

1. The parties involved.

2. The objectives of the joint venture.

3. Financial contributions you will each make whether you will transfer any assets or employees to the joint venture.

4. Intellectual property developed by the participants in the joint venture.

5. Day to day management of finances, responsibilities and processes to be followed.

6. Dispute resolution, how any disagreements between the parties will be resolved.

7. How if necessary the joint venture can be terminated.

8. The use of confidentiality or non-disclosure agreements is also recommended to protect the parties when disclosing sensitive commercial secrets or confidential information.

Chapter 24: Tips for Going Further, Faster with Joint Venture

While some entrepreneurs may be hesitant to partner with other companies due to fear of misalignment, not a balanced relationship or a branding disaster, it can actually be quite beneficial if done correctly. Forming the right joint venture can increase your efforts in two essential areas of the business; credibility and distribution.

For those thinking of forming a joint venture, here are a few pieces of advice.

1. Identify opportunities. Any company can come up with a list of the top 100 partners they would love to work with in under an hour.

The trick is to identify what you can offer and align these incentives with a company that fills one of your needs. Look for companies that might be able to bring in valuable customers, credibility or links, among other resources. The key is looking for a partner with a matched vision and wants more than just a transactional relationship. Chances are you are going to be working closely with these companies for extended periods of time, so it's in everyone's best interest to make sure the spirit, vision and culture are all aligned.

2. Use partnerships to build momentum. Whether you are talking to customers, investors or other potential partners, you need credibility to gain leverage. Latching on to a bigger, well-known brand through a mutually beneficial partnership is a way to quickly build your own brand and credibility. Plus, your company can use the momentum gained from one partnership or deal to leverage another.

3. Make sure you have the required resources. Like any major function of your business, you need to allocate first-class resources to your joint venture. This means that both sides need to have the capital, people power and leadership in place to be able to devote time, energy and money into the partnership. Make sure your company fulfils these obligations.

That said, be aware that a majority of joint ventures won't exactly plan out the way you want them too. Needs change, company's pivot; it just happens.

4. Negotiate your terms and stay the course. Often with young start-ups in relationships with larger, more established companies, the bigger business uses its weight to get what it want. This leaves the smaller company in an uncomfortable position where they can lose track of their own growth. Don't let this happen to you.

It is essential to make sure the deal is structured in a way that lets you maintain control of your company.

As a general rule, it's best to stay away from granting exclusivity to one company or another. You don't want to back yourself into a corner that you can't escape in the long run.

I always evaluate joint venture pragmatically, taking them on a case-by-case basis. If the partnership fits, incentives are aligned and the cultures match, you might be on the cusp of securing the big partnership that takes your company out of the basement and into the world.

Chapter 25: Advantages and Disadvantage of a Joint Venture

There are many good business and accounting reasons to participate in a Joint Venture (often shortened JV). Partnering with a business that has complementary abilities and resources, such as finance, distribution channels, or technology, makes good sense. These are just some of the reasons partnerships formed by joint venture are becoming increasingly popular.

A joint venture is a strategic alliance between two or more individuals or entities to engage in a specific project or undertaking. Partnerships and joint ventures can be similar but in fact can have significantly different implications for those involved. A partnership usually involves a continuing, long-term business relationship, whereas a joint venture can be based on a single business project.

Parties enter Joint Ventures to gain individual benefits, usually a share of the project objective. This may be to develop a product or intellectual property rather than joint or collective profits, as is the case with a general or limited partnership.

A joint venture, like a general partnership is not a separate legal entity. Revenues, expenses and asset ownership usually flow through the joint venture to the participants, since the joint venture itself has no legal status. Once the Joint venture has met its goals the entity ceases to exist.

Advantages of forming a Joint Venture.

1. Provide companies with the opportunity to gain new capacity and expertise.

2. Allow companies to enter related businesses or new geographic markets or gain new technological knowledge.

3. Access to greater resources, including specialised staff and technology.

4. Sharing of risks with a venture partner.

5. Joint ventures can be flexible. For example, a joint venture can have a limited life span and only cover part of what you do, thus limiting both your commitment and the business' exposure.

6. In the era of divestiture and consolidation, JV's offer a creative way for companies to exit from non-core businesses.

7. Companies can gradually separate a business from the rest of the organisation, and eventually, sell it to the other parent company. Roughly 80% of all joint ventures end in a sale by one partner to the other.

The Disadvantages of Joint Ventures

It takes time and effort to build the right relationship and partnering with another business can be challenging. Problems are likely to arise if:

1. The objectives of the venture are not 100 per cent clear and communicated to everyone involved.

2. There is an imbalance in levels of expertise, investment or assets brought into the venture by the different partners.

3. Different cultures and management styles result in poor integration and co-operation.

4. The partners don't provide enough leadership and support in the early stages.

5. Success in a joint venture depends on thorough research and analysis of the objectives.

Embarking on a Joint Venture can represent a significant reconstruction to your business; however favourable it may be to your potential for growth, it needs to fit with your overall business strategy.

It's important to review your business strategy before committing to a joint venture. This should help you define what you can sensibly expect. In fact, you might decide there are better ways to achieve your business aims.

You may also want to study what similar businesses are doing, particular those that operate in similar markets to yours. Seeing how they use joint ventures could help you decide on the best approach for your business. At the same time, you could try to identify the skills they use to partner successfully.

You can benefit from studying your own enterprise. Be realistic about your strengths and weaknesses; consider performing strengths, weaknesses, opportunities and threats analysis (swot) to identify whether the two businesses are compatible. You will almost certainly want to identify a joint venture partner that complements your own skills and failings.

Remember to consider the employees' perspective and bear in mind that people can feel threatened by a joint venture. It may be difficult to foster effective working relationships if your partner has a different way of doing business.

When embarking on a joint venture it's imperative to have your understanding in writing. You should set out the terms and conditions agreed upon in a written contract, this will help prevent misunderstandings and provide both parties with strong legal recourse in the event the other party fails to fulfil its obligations while under contract.

Chapter 26: Making the Most Out of a Joint Venture

A joint venture is a popular way for most companies to raise their profit margins and to reduce risks involved in going into business. Most likely you've tallied up the pros and cons and have decided to go into joint venture to develop your business; however, now that you've got yourself a partner and are going into business with him or her, what should you be aiming for? Most people hit a dead end when this comes up. This chapter aim to help you get over that hump. Being a part in a joint venture is a great way for a business to develop a healthy profit margin but you have to know how to maximize the relationship between you and your partner. It can be a rocky road ahead but these few pieces of advice should help out a bit.

First of all, look out for your interests. Yes, your maybe partners but this doesn't mean that you should just merely cooperate like sheep. Take note of what can benefit you in your business dealings; try to build your company's strength while also shoring up your partnership.

This usually comes in the form of developing know-how and experience; remember that mostly joint ventures are a limited and you may eventually have to break off your relationship with your partner. It would be good to have people in your ranks that knows about some of the things that are usually out of your hands. Building up contacts in the market are also a good idea; cultivating your own stable of business appointments can help a lot when you decide to go your separate ways.

Secondly, look at what you are putting into your partnership. Always remember that a joint venture is a partnership. Like a marriage, there should be an equal division of work; having your partner doing the easy part of the operation or not putting in the same amount of effort or resources into the business as you are will be detrimental to your company's future financial health. Take notice of such disparities and make your partner pay attention to it. Having your partner carry his own weight is essential for success in a joint venture.

Thirdly, pay attention to the venture itself. A joint venture is like an independent business. You should take a look at its profit margins and losses. Make sure that you are in the black and are well aware of the market forces that may affect your partnership. You should also pay attention to the "joint" part of a joint venture; make sure your relationship with your JV partner is both cordial and stable; this can make or break the partnership.

Remember that your partner is also looking at the bottom-line and it would be best to work together to achieve that. There you go; a few tips on helping you get the most out of your joint venture. Remember to always keep them in mind and you will have a success in your hands in no time.

Chapter 27: Examples of Joint Ventures

It is very unlikely that Shell-MS and BP, United Glass (Owens-Illinois and Distillers), British Aircraft Corporation (GEC and Vickers) or Mitsubishi Heavy Industries and Chrysler would have taken this route unless it provided them with optimum profitability.

It was by means of a joint venture that Shell broke into the Italian petrochemical industry; supplying the fluids which Montecatini, strong in research and management, needed and could not obtain in the difficult Italian capital market. Also, General Electric took advantage of Machines Bull's lack of working capital to supply this need and, with Bull's first-class marketing set-up, formed a viable joint venture.

Mitsubishi Heavy Industries, having been concerned entirely with engineering, while the Mitsubishi group's own trading company handled all its marketing, first entered joint ventures with Caterpillar Tractor and then Borg-Warner to market earth-moving equipment and industrial refrigeration equipment, respectively. In the US Mitsubishi Heavy Industries thus benefited from its partners' expertise in marketing and after-sales service. Now, the motor vehicles division of Mitsubishi having been formed into a separate company, a joint venture has been set up with Chrysler in which the latter began with 15 per cent participation and an option to increase this to 35 per cent. Not only is the company currently exporting over 4,000 units a month to America, but sales in Japan have also increased greatly.

A good example of a company opting for a joint venture in an overseas market in which it was forbidden to have a majority shareholding, yet effectively controlling the operation despite this, was provided by Corning Glass in India. In return for cash investment was allowed 39 per cent and for its technical contribution a further 10 per cent. Of the remaining 5 per cent, half was taken up by the Indian partner and half put on the stock market. Thus, despite its minority position, Corning Glass was in the seat of power because 25.5 per cent of the possible vote against it was widely spread.

Perhaps the most friendly way of handling a joint venture is to set up two companies, one to manufacture and one to market, with the equity divided 51/49 per cent and 49/51 per cent respectively, between the partners. In the cleaning industry, which, in addition to contract cleaning firms, embraces the manufacture of machines, chemical products, and a constantly growing range of mops, buckets, wringers and equipment trolleys of increasing sophistication for the cleaning and maintenance of industrial, institutional and hospital premises, an interesting recent joint venture has been established on these lines.

The biggest contract cleaning organization in the world is Danish and employs 30,000 cleaning staff in Scandinavia alone. This company, Der Danske Rengring Service, also manufactures a range of cleaning equipment under the name of Darenas and owns another Danish company manufacturing industrial chemical cleaning products. Der Danske Rengring Service is now engaged on a series of joint ventures with Electrolux to cover both contract cleaning and the manufacturing and supply of machines and other cleaning products. Where a contract cleaning business is established, the Danish partner holds 51 per cent and Electrolux 49 per cent of the equity. Where a marketing operation is set up, the shareholding ratio is reversed. By this means, a world-wide comprehensive cleaning and marketing operation has been made possible.

The construction of a joint venture agreement offers wide scope for the exercise of negotiating skill, and when it is between partners from different countries it can be one of the most worthwhile contributions marketing executives can make to international relations. The essential qualities, in addition to experience and subtlety in this type of bargaining, are the ability to remain unruffled, to be resilient and to be tolerant without being weak. Perhaps, above all, toughness is needed, for the long-term implications of a joint venture mean that a negotiator is committing his company to a future in which its position must be strong from the outset.

There are many control techniques open to those who enter joint ventures, in addition to those already listed. These may be established through patent and trademark rights; rotating chairmanship of the joint company (as in the Italian venture by Finsider and US Steel); agreements for continuing contributions of know-how, production, or service; or an option agreement. The last has two uses; firstly, to enable the partner who enjoys it to increase his equity by an agreed amount in the future; secondly as a threat that he will do so if the other partner does not comply with his wishes should a confrontation arise. Monsanto is a good example of a company that has obtained, and exercised, equity options on more than one occasion in its European joint ventures.

As a final recommendation, an international joint venture agreement should provide that disputes between the partners will be decided in a third country, to ensure impartiality; Switzerland, or the International Court at The Hague are good choices.

Chapter 28: Why Big Firms Form Joint Ventures

Nestle SA and Colgate-Palmolive formed a joint venture to develop and sell candy that can produce plague and clean teeth. IBM and Lenovo Group also formed a joint venture. IBM sold its PC Division to the China-based company that would make the latter the third world's largest PC maker. Skype Software of Denmark and Tom Online of China developed a joint venture to distribute a simplified version of Skype's VOIP. Is joint ventures business hype or a way to achieve business strategies? Here are the reasons why many big business firms form joint ventures.

1. To develop new products: Examples of functional confectionary products are gum and candy that have health and beauty benefits. Sales of these products are growing by over 6 percent each year which is twice the growth rate of standard gum and candy. Nestle SA had no functional confectionary products prior to its joint venture with Colgate-Palmolive. Cadbury Schweppes, PLC's Adams, and Wm. Wrigley Jr. dominate the functional confectionery segment.

2. Allow companies to improve communications and networking: In today's business environment joint ventures are most appropriate to topple scarce resources, rapid rates of technological change, and rising capital requirements.

3. Effective way to enhance corporate growth: Strategic partnering like joint ventures are very important to enhance corporate growth. Eli Lilly host partnership training classes for their managers and partners. Starbucks joint venture with China's President Coffee and opened hundreds of new branches in China. Eli Lilly and Starbucks are just two of the 10,000 joint ventures formed annually.

4. Globalization: A major reason why firms are using joint ventures as a means to achieve business strategies is globalization. International joint ventures are very common today; one good example is Wal-Mart's successful joint venture with Mexico's Cifra. Such alliance indicates how a domestic firm can benefit immensely by partnering with a foreign company to gain a global presence.

5. Technology: The Internet paved the way and legitimized the need for partnership and alliances. Corporate growth cannot happen without the help of state-of-the-art technologies.

How can a company determine if a joint venture is the best business strategy to pursue? Here are six guidelines.

1. When synergistically combining unique advantages like closed ownership of a privately owned company and access to stock issuances as a source of capital of a publicly owned company results to enhanced corporate growth, access to new technologies, greater market feedback and more long-term positive consequences.

2. When a joint venture provides the opportunity to reduce risk.

3. When the distinct competencies of participants complement with each other well.

4. When projects are profitable.

5. When two or more firms have difficulty in competing with larger firm.

6. When there exist needs to introduce a new technology quickly.

Other recent joint ventures not mentioned previously include Wachovia Brokerage and Prudential Brokerage. In the U.S. and Europe today, firms are acquiring foreign companies and forming joint ventures with foreign firms, and foreign firms are also acquiring U.S. and European companies and forming joint ventures with U.S. and European firms.

Chapter 29: Joint Venture Frequently Ask Questions

1. What kinds of joint ventures are there?

The term joint venture is most commonly used to describe an arrangement where two (or more) businesses create a separate joint venture business. But any kind of collaboration with another company could be described as a joint venture.

For example:
  a) Contractual arrangements such as entering into a distribution agreement.
  b) Setting up a separate joint venture company to carry out a specific (and often finite) project such as development of a new product.
  c) Forming a partnership.
  d) Merging two businesses.

Joint ventures generally involve some sharing of resources and risks.

2. What is the best way to structure a joint venture?

A common and flexible solution is to form a separate limited company for the joint venture. Among other advantages, this allows you to insulate yourself from liability should the joint venture become insolvent, because your liability as a shareholder is limited to the amount you have agreed to pay for your shares; however, this is not always the best solution.

If you will be transferring significant assets into the joint venture, forming a separate company can have unwanted tax consequences. An alternative can be to form a partnership or a limited liability partnership. An appropriate partnership structure may minimise potential tax liabilities.

If you do not require management involvement in the joint venture, it may be best to use contractual arrangements rather than to create a separate joint venture entity. For example, an inventor could simply license their intellectual property rights in their invention to another business to exploit.

3. What issues do I need to consider when looking for a joint venture partner?

Normally, you will be looking for a partner with complementary strengths. For example, you might want to find a company with a distribution network through which you can market your product or with financial resources to invest in developing your intellectual property, such as an invention, a copyright work such as a film or book or a design.

As well as your own requirements, think about what your partner will be hoping to get from the venture. You will need to be able to agree objectives that suit both of you. You will also need to reach agreement on a whole range of other issues.

Bear in mind that, sooner or later, the joint venture may come to an end. This can make it difficult to collaborate with a competitor or with a business that is likely to compete with you in the future.

4. What are the main issues that need to be agreed with a joint venture partner?

Issues to be considered include:
   a) The structure of the joint venture.
   b) What the joint venture's objectives are; how it will be managed.
   c) How it will be financed and what will happen if further funding is needed in the future.
   d) What assets, including intellectual property, you will each contribute.
   e) Who will work for the new venture.
   f) What information will be reported to you.
   g) How profits will be shared.
   h) Who will own any intellectual property created by the joint venture.
   i) How any disputes between the joint venture partners will be handled.
   j) What exit routes will be available if you want to realise your investment in the joint venture.

All the key issues need to be covered by appropriate agreements.

5. Does forming a joint venture need regulatory approval?

In general, no; however, a joint venture may raise competition issues, if, for example, the joint venture will have a significant market share. In circumstances such as this, the joint venture may be subject to review by the Competition and Markets Authority and it can be a good idea to seek guidance from the outset.

6. Is collaborating with a competitor allowed by competition law?

Competition law aims to prevent collaborations that reduce competition. In most cases, this only applies if you and your joint venture partner have a combined market share of more than 25%.

Some forms of collaboration are strictly prohibited in any circumstances, for example, agreements to fix prices or to share markets. On the other hand, there are some limited exceptions that can, for example, allow collaboration on research and development.

Competition law is complex. If in any doubt, take legal advice.

7. Is agreeing not to compete with a joint venture allowed by competition law?

In general, and to the extent that the agreement is directly necessary to the joint venture, collaborators in a joint venture can agree not to compete with it. This does not, however, cover agreements that include elements such as price fixing or sharing markets.

As with other aspects of competition law, take advice if you are in any doubt.

8. How do I protect myself while we are negotiating a joint venture?

Normally, each party signs a confidentiality agreement. This requires them not to disclose any of your confidential information they learn in the course of negotiations, nor use it to your detriment.

It can also be a good idea to sign a memorandum of understanding at an early stage in the negotiations. This represents a commitment to the deal and agreement in principle on the main points.

9. What due diligence is needed?

Due diligence will include checking your joint venture partner's legal status, that they have the right to enter the joint venture, that they own assets they will be putting into the joint venture and so on.

More broadly, due diligence aims to ensure any agreements you enter into are valid and to minimise risk of future legal problems.

10. What legal agreements will we need to put in place?

If you are forming a new joint venture company, a shareholders' agreement and the new company's articles of association are crucial.

Points that may be covered in these or in separate agreements include:

a) The financing arrangements for the joint venture.
b) Agreements not to compete with the joint venture.
c) Arrangements for licensing or transferring intellectual property in inventions, brands, designs or copyright works such as plans or manuals to the joint venture.
d) Agreements on any services or supplies you will provide to the joint venture.
e) Confidentiality agreements.
f) How any disputes will be handled.
g) How the partners can exit the joint venture.
h) Any agreements that will continue after the joint venture is terminated

11. What are the tax consequences of transferring assets into a joint venture?

The transfer of assets may be subject to stamp duty and capital gains tax liability if the asset has increased in value since it was originally acquired.

It may be possible to structure the transaction in a way that reduces the tax consequences, for example, by giving the joint venture the right to use the assets rather than transferring ownership.

This is a complex area. If you will be transferring assets of any significant value, take specialist tax advice.

12. What are the implications of putting employees into a joint venture?

It depends on how the employees are transferred and what their existing employment contracts say.

Employees could continue to be employed by you, but be seconded to the venture. Employees may be able to claim constructive unfair dismissal if, for example, they are required to relocate and do not wish to do so.

Alternatively, a business including the employees working in it might be transferred into the joint venture. The employees' existing contractual rights will be protected. Again, employees might be able to claim unfair dismissal depending upon the circumstances of transfer. The Transfer of Undertakings (Protection of Employees) Regulations, which are designed to protect employees if the business they work in is acquired by a new owner, must be considered at all times and specialist employment advice should be taken.

Thirdly, an employee could be offered the opportunity to resign and take up a new job with the joint venture. Depending on the ownership of the joint venture, some of the employee's rights (such as continuous service) under the existing employment contract might be protected.

As with most employment matters, you can minimise the likelihood of any dispute by discussing and negotiating your plans with the employees involved.

13. How do we handle the intellectual property we contribute to the joint venture and any intellectual property created by the joint venture?

A joint venture may need to use intellectual property owned by one or more of the collaborators setting up the joint venture, such as brands, inventions, database rights, designs or copyright works such as plans, blueprints, manuals, etc.

Usually you would grant (or sell) the joint venture a licence to use your intellectual property. The licence will specify what rights and restrictions there are, for example, if the joint venture is only allowed to use your intellectual property within a certain territory. A licence, as opposed to a sale, may be more suitable to protect the ownership of intellectual property if the joint venture is not successful.

You will also need to ensure there is clear agreement on the ownership of any new intellectual property created by the joint venture. Care needs to be taken over what will happen if the joint venture modifies your intellectual property, for example, by developing an improved version of a patented product. Otherwise, over time you could lose ownership of the modified intellectual property to the joint venture.

14. How do we value the contribution each of us makes to the joint venture?

There may be various indicators that guide you in valuing your contribution, for example, the replacement cost of assets you contribute, but, ultimately, it is a matter for negotiation.

15. How much control will I have over the joint venture?

Your degree of control depends on what has been agreed. When a new joint venture company is formed, it is common practice for the shareholders' agreement to include clauses relating to each party's rights to appoint directors, how decisions will be taken and so on. A similar agreement can be put in place if the joint venture is structured in some other way, such as a partnership.

Often joint venture partners want deadlock, with each having the right to veto the actions of the joint venture. You will need to agree how you will escape from the deadlock if it goes on too long. For example, you might decide you will wind the joint venture up if there is a deadlock or that one party will buy the other out at a fair price.

16. What accounting and other information do I need to receive?

You will usually want to receive the same sort of information as you do within your own company; management accounts; copies of board briefings; minutes of board meetings; and so on.

If you or one of your colleagues is a director of the joint venture company, you would normally have easy access to the information you require. In any case, your rights to information should be specified in the shareholders' agreement.

17. How do we take profits from the joint venture?

Profits from joint venture companies are commonly distributed through dividends. Of course, the ability of the joint venture to pay dividends will depend on its cash-flow position. Depending on the circumstances, there may also be other more tax-effective ways of realising part of the value of your investment in the joint venture.

Where a joint venture is structured as a partnership, profits are automatically shared between the partners as specified in the partnership agreement. The partnership agreement should also specify what cash payments partners can take from the partnership.

If there is no separate joint venture entity, there will be no need to 'take' profits from the joint venture; the profits will in any case arise within your (or your joint venture partner's) business.

18. What is the best way to terminate a joint venture?

Usually, one partner will buy out the other. The key is to plan for the termination of the joint venture from the outset. For example, the original agreement can include provisions that allow you to force your partner either to sell you their stake or to purchase your stake from you.

19. Will I be liable if the joint venture becomes insolvent?

If the joint venture that becomes insolvent is a limited company, you will not normally be liable as a shareholder, because your liability for its debts is limited to the amount you have agreed to pay for your shares in the joint venture company. You will, however, be liable if you have personally guaranteed the joint venture company's debts. If the joint venture is structured as a partnership, your liability will depend on exactly how this has been done.

Even where you are not liable, there can be indirect effects on your business. For example, your image may be affected if you are associated with the joint venture.

Chapter 30: Joint venture checklist

A checklist can be useful when you are planning a joint venture.

1. Is your business prepared?

To check whether your business is ready for a joint venture, you should:
- a) Research the activities of other businesses in this area.
- b) Carry out a SWOT (strengths, weaknesses, opportunities and threats) analysis of your business.
- c) Compare your working methods with those of potential partners.
- d) Consult your employees to find out their feelings about a joint venture.

2. Choosing the right partner

When choosing a joint venture partner, you should consider:
- a) Existing customers and suppliers, competitors and professional associates as partners.
- b) Whether the culture of a proposed partner fits with that of your organisation.
- c) Whether the finances of the proposed partner organisation are sound.
- d) Potential for overseas sales or activities.

3. Finance

You should prepare the following documents for a joint venture:
    a) Business plan.
    b) Marketing plan.
    c) Cash-flow projection.

Each partner should agree who is investing what, and in what form - e.g. cash or other assets.

If external funding is needed, the partners should agree:
    a) Sources of funding, e.g. a share issue.
    b) Who will borrow the funds.
    c) How the borrowing will be guaranteed.

Arrangements for profit and loss should be agreed, e.g.:
    a) How any profits or losses should be divided.
    b) How capital gains or losses should be divided.
    c) Whether one partner will be paid for providing services, other than through a share of profits

4. Implementing a joint venture

When you are ready to implement a joint venture, you should make a joint venture agreement including:
    a) Clear business objectives.
    b) Communication arrangements between organisations/teams.
    c) Financial arrangements.
    d) Protection of your interests, e.g. trade secrets.

e) Day-to-day and strategic decision making.
f) Whether either party can pursue other business during the joint venture.
g) Dispute resolution procedures.

5. Decide on a legal structure for your joint venture, e.g:

a) Contractual co-operation for a defined project.
b) Partnership or unlimited partnership.
c) Limited liability company.
d) Full merger of the two organisations.

Bank account arrangements will depend on the legal model chosen, although a new account can be set up for a single project. You should agree:
a) In whose name account(s) are set up.
b) Arrangements for depositing or withdrawing funds, including co-signatories.

6. Sourcing business together

You should agree in advance which organisation has responsibility for:
a) Sales activities.
b) Marketing activities.
c) New business generation

Such arrangements should be specified in the joint venture business and marketing plans.

7. Terminating the joint venture

The agreement needs to make provision for terminating the agreement, covering:
a) Termination procedure.
b) Ownership of assets in the joint venture.
c) Allocation of any liabilities resulting from the joint venture.

Chapter 31: Terminating a Joint Venture and the Consequences

The enthusiasm and shared commercial goals which brought the joint venture participants together can dissipate for various reasons.

It is possible that a joint venture will terminate as a result of an event of default. A well-crafted joint venture agreement (JVA) will specify the obligations of the joint venture parties and will clearly and accurately express those circumstances or events which constitute an 'event of default'. Commonly encountered event of default scenarios include:

a) Insolvency of one party (or possibly its parent company).
b) Material or persistent breach of the JVA.
c) Change of control of a joint venture party (particularly if the party acquiring control is a competitor of the other joint venture party), or.
d) An attempted transfer of a party's interest in the joint venture other than in accordance with the JVA.

If an event of default occurs and the JVA does not contain any specific contractual remedies, then the innocent party may terminate and seek damages. Given the difficulty in quantifying the 'loss' suffered, the JVA may contain a default 'put and call' mechanism, which allows the innocent party either.

a) To acquire the shares of the defaulting party at a discount to fair value (although care should be taken to ensure that the discount is not so great as to constitute a 'penalty' and, as a result, unenforceable) or
b) To sell its shares to the defaulting party at a premium to fair value (the premium acting as a deterrent to a party looking to engineer a default with a view to being bought out).

Fixed term or specific objective

Some joint ventures are established for a fixed term or for a specific objective. Once the term has expired, or the objective has been achieved, the joint venture automatically terminates, with the joint venture wound up and any assets distributed between the joint venture parties.

Termination as a result of an exit event

Joint ventures may come to an end simply through the sale of one or all parties' interests in the joint venture.

Termination due to deadlock

It is possible that, as a result of a deadlock, parties may be unwilling or unable to continue with the joint venture, resulting in an exit being sought.

Key considerations when terminating a joint venture

We are often asked to advise on the key issues to consider when a party is contemplating bringing a joint venture to an end. In most instances, the business of the joint venture will continue and one party will simply acquire the joint venture completely and go it alone, on the basis that the interests of neither party are likely to be served if the business is broken up and the assets liquidated or a sale forced upon the parties. It is therefore from this angle that we have compiled the following list of top ten considerations. The key factors will, of course, vary depending on the structure of the joint venture.

1. Change of control

The joint venture company is likely to have entered into a number of commercial contracts with suppliers or customers. These contracts may provide that they can be renegotiated or terminated if there is a change in control or ownership of the joint venture company. These contracts should be identified prior to terminating the joint venture and appropriate consents obtained. Indeed, when negotiating such contacts, the definition of 'change of control' should exclude the situation where one of the joint venture participants simply acquires outright control.

2. Risk profile

A joint venture is a popular vehicle for commercial activity in the Energy and Natural Resources sector due to the inherent uncertainty and risk associated with many types of energy projects. The number of variables, as well as the often significant capital requirements, particularly in offshore projects, means that it is often preferable for risk to be spread among one or more parties.

When termination of a joint venture occurs in circumstances where one party continues the business of the joint venture, then they do so with increased risk and will ultimately bear the sole risk of failure. A full and thorough risk assessment of the joint venture business should be carried out and measures taken to de-risk the venture to a suitable level, which may entail seeking a new partner.

3. Experience

In addition to the spreading of risk, experience will be a key determinant in selecting a joint venture partner at the outset. A party seeking to terminate a joint venture by buying out its joint venture partner will need to assess whether it alone has the requisite knowledge and experience to achieve the objectives of the joint venture. This will be material where there is a shortage of expertise in the particular field such as joint ventures involved in unconventional gas.

4. Financial considerations

If, as part of the termination, one party will acquire the other party's interest then the acquirer should ensure that appropriate funding is in place for the initial purchase, which may require entering into capital/debt markets or even securing a new partner. It is also important to understand any existing finance provided to the joint venture by the exiting party, since this will undoubtedly require to be dealt with as part of the exit. If the exiting party requires its loans to the joint venture to be repaid, the remaining party should carefully consider its ability to refinance that debt.

5. On-going funding

It is also of critical importance that the on-going CAPEX and OPEX requirements of the joint venture business are understood to ensure termination does not result in a funding gap. The outgoing partner may also have granted a parent company guarantee in respect of the joint venture business, which may need to be replaced.

6. Assets

The joint venture may use assets, such as intellectual property or IT, which are owned by the exiting party. Consideration should be given as to how the joint venture business will operate without these assets or whether viable alternatives exist. If no reasonable alternatives exist then, as part of the exit, contracts will have to be put in place with the exiting party to ensure continued use (e.g. transitional arrangements, whether long term or for an appropriate run off period). Naturally these arrangements will come at a cost, which should be factored into the exit negotiations.

7. Goodwill protection

A well-drafted joint venture agreement (JVA) will include controls on the use of confidential information shared for the purposes of the joint venture, as well as restrictive covenants which seek to protect the goodwill of the joint venture business. These provisions are likely to continue beyond termination of the joint venture, so the parties must fully appreciate what they can and cannot do following termination. An existing party will not want to discover that its core business is in fact caught by the non-compete restrictions within the JVA.

8. Staff

Responsibility for staff employed by the joint venture, either permanent or on secondment, can be problematic. Seconded staff are likely to return to their original employer, which may leave the joint venture under resourced. Alternatively, if the joint venture parties do not intend to integrate staff back into the parent businesses, the costs and related effects of redundancies will need to be considered.

9. Pensions

Any pension arrangements which have been put in place for the joint venture staff will merit consideration. Required actions will depend on whether the staff will transfer to another employer or be made redundant and also on the nature of the arrangements in place. The joint venture may have set up its own pension arrangements or used those of a joint venture party. The nature of the benefits provided by the arrangement will be relevant. A defined benefit arrangement with a funding deficit could have significant cost implications.

10. Tax implications

Tax implications will be a major consideration in deciding which method of termination is most appropriate for a specific joint venture. This chapter is based on the assumption that the joint venture is a limited liability company. In this case, the transfer of assets back to the joint venture parties on the winding up of the vehicle may give rise to a corporation tax charge (as well as stamp duty and VAT depending on the type of asset). The sale of shares in the joint venture by a joint venture partner may qualify for Substantial Shareholding Exemption, but would otherwise result in a corporation tax charge. It is also possible for a joint venture to be established as a partnership in which case the transfer of assets back to the partners can give rise to capital gains tax charges. Other taxes can apply depending on the assets and circumstances involved.

Do your homework

As is evident from the above, the effect of a termination event on the business of a joint venture can be far reaching. Joint venture parties should consider the wide range of commercial, operational, legal and practical issues which could arise as a result of terminating a joint venture. Indeed, joint venture parties would be well advised to carry out thorough

due diligence in advance of any termination to ensure, where the intention is to continue the business, that:
a) The joint venture is sustainable.
b) The value of the joint venture business will not be materially eroded.
c) There are no unwanted surprises following termination.

Chapter 32: Conclusion

Joint ventures are important in business. Getting into one is a way for most companies to make the most of their resources without having to risk much and raise a lot of capital. This is especially true for young companies who are just starting their operations and are still testing the waters.

But as much as it is one viable idea for businesses, it is not always beneficial. In fact, out of the many who attempt to get into a joint venture, only a few manages to really survive the first five years. This is not because of the "joint venture" per se but because the partners or the partner companies are incompatible.

That is actually the first rule that you should know when opting for a joint venture. Just because a company fits your needs-criteria does not mean that it is already a perfect fit to you or your company for a joint venture. You see, a company may provide the service, the product or the technology that you need for a project but if they are not a company that you trust, partnering with them may mean suicide for you. There are a lot of smaller companies who have been eaten up by big companies because they made the mistake of getting into joint ventures with those industrial sharks.

Choose your partner well. preferably it should be someone or a company that is similar to you in stature or if ever slightly smaller or bigger. Partnering with a big company may give you instant access but it can be a problem for you in the long run. The partner should be trustworthy and whose work ethic coincides with how you do business. If you find a company who is comfortable in testing the laws and you can't, it will be a disaster. It is better not to start the partnership at all than to bail out of an agreement.

Another important consideration is to make sure that everything is in writing. That way, you can be sure that everybody will be doing their part. It is not impossible for people to slack off especially when they know that another partner can take over their responsibilities for them. This can be a huge problem and may create discord among in the group.

Another vital thing that you have to look into is the profit sharing and the contribution of each of the partners to the enterprise. This is perhaps the most important aspect of the joint venture because this is after all what all these companies are after. Although the partners are primarily giving something to the joint venture, some will have more contributions than others. It is important that you check all these and make sure that you have the profits and the compensation distributed to the partners fairly.

Take note, the word is fairly and not equally. This means that distributing the profits equally to all partners is not the way to go. It should be distributed to the partners according to their contributions to the joint venture.

Good Luck!!

Printed in Great Britain
by Amazon